Nichola

You Can Still Make a Killing

Methuen Drama

Published by Methuen Drama

Methuen Drama, an imprint of Bloomsbury Publishing Plc

1 3 5 7 9 10 8 6 4 2

Methuen Drama
Bloomsbury Publishing Plc
50 Bedford Square
London WC1B 3DP
www.methuendrama.com

Copyright © Nicholas Pierpan 2012

The right of Nicholas Pierpan to be identified as the author
of this work has been asserted by him in accordance
with the Copyright, Designs and Patents Act 1988

ISBN: 978 1 408 18560 5

A CIP catalogue record for this book is available from the British Library

Available in the USA from Bloomsbury Academic & Professional,
175 Fifth Avenue/3rd Floor, New York, NY 10010.
www.BloomsburyAcademicUSA.com

Typeset by Country Setting, Kingsdown, Kent

Rix Productions and Mimi Poskitt
present the world premiere of

YOU CAN STILL
MAKE A KILLING

by
Nicholas Pierpan

This production was first performed
at Southwark Playhouse, London, on 10 October 2012

The Actors

in alphabetical order

Emma	**Alecky Blythe**
Fen Knowles	**Kellie Bright**
Andrezj	**Max Calandrew**
Edward Knowles	**Tim Delap**
Sir Roger Glynn	**Robert Gwilym**
Jack Tilly	**Ben Lee**
Interviewer / Jack's Lawyer / Paula	**Claire Lichie**
Chris	**William Mannering**
Linda Tilly	**Marianne Oldham**
Henry	**David Partridge**
Kim Lopez	**Elexi Walker**

The Team

Director	**Matthew Dunster**
Designer	**Alison McDowall**
Lighting Designer	**Chloe Kenward**
Sound Designer	**Emma Laxton**
Casting Director	**Sue Needleman**
Hair	**Anna Morena**
Voice	**Michaela Kennen**
Assistant Director	**Samuel Wood**
Stage Manager	**Jenny Grand**
Rehearsal Assistant	**Eliza Turner**
Press Representative	**Susie Safavi** (020 7407 0234)

This production has been made possible
through the generous support of Douglas Kennedy
and those donors who wish to remain anonymous.

Biographies

Nicholas Pierpan

Nicholas Pierpan is a two-time winner of the Cameron Mackintosh Award for New Writing. His play *The Maddening Rain*, also directed by Matthew Dunster, premiered at the Old Red Lion in 2010 to critical acclaim; it then toured the UK before going to New York City as part of the 2011 *Brits Off Broadway* Festival. *Devolution* was a finalist for the 2009 Yale Drama Prize in the US (judged by Sir David Hare) and *Too Much the Sun* was published by Samuel French in 2008. He has recently had short plays produced with *The Miniaturists* and the Off Cuts Festival as well as a full-length production of *The Problem with the Seventh Year* at Theatre Ulm (Germany). He won the 2009 BAFTA/Script Factory Serious Screenwriting Award, and was selected for the 2010 BBC Sparks Radio Residency. His radio plays have been broadcast on BBC Radio 3, Radio 4 and Radio 7.

Matthew Dunster | Director

Directing credits include: *The Sacred Flame* (English Touring Theatre), *A Midsummer Night's Dream* (Open Air Theatre, Regent's Park), *Mogadishu* (Lyric Theatre, Hammersmith and Royal Exchange - nominated for Olivier Award for Outstanding Achievement In An Affiliate Theatre), *The Maddening Rain* (Soho Theatre), *Love the Sinner* (National Theatre), *The Fahrenheit Twins* (Barbican), *Dr Faustus, Troilus and Cressida, The Frontline* (Shakespeare's Globe), *Saturday Night and Sunday Morning, Macbeth, 1984* (Royal Exchange Theatre), *You Can See The Hills, Love and Money* (Royal Exchange Theatre and Young Vic - nominated for Olivier Award for Outstanding Achievement In An Affiliate Theatre), *Testing the Echo* (Out of Joint), *Some Voices, The Member of the Wedding* (Young Vic), Cruising (Bush Theatre), *Project B, Project D: I'm Mediocre, The Work, Port Authority* (Liverpool Everyman).

As well as being a writer and actor, Matthew was also a founding member of both Quarantine and The Work theatre companies. He was an Associate Director of the Young Vic for four years and is currently an Associate Artist.

Alison McDowall | Designer

Theatre designs include: *The Ugly Sisters* (Northern Stage's venue St.Stephens, Edinburgh), *Brightest and Best* (The Half Moon Theatre), *The Maddening Rain* (Old Red Lion, The Soho Theatre, 59E59 Theatre, New York), *The Quick* (The Tristan Bates Theatre), *A Just Act Production* (Clean Break Theatre Company, UK prison tour), *Heartspeak* (Studio K, The Arcola).

Theatre as an associate designer includes: *Troilus and Cressida* (The Globe), *Love the Sinner* (The National Theatre), *The London Eye Mystery* (The Unicorn), *Beasts and Beauties* (Hampstead Theatre).

Opera as an associate designer: *Zaide* (Sadler's Well's Theatre).

Chloe Kenward | Lighting Designer

Theatre includes: *La Boheme*, *Aesop's Fables*, *The Ragged Trousered Philanthropists*, (Isango Ensemble, Hackney Empire), *Mack and Mabel* (Greenwich Playhouse), *The Quick* (Tristan Bates Theatre), *Frank and Ferdinand* (ICT, Soho Theatre NT Connections), *Romeo and Juliet*, (Box Clever, UK Tour), *Primary Voices* (Quicksilver, New Diorama Theatre), *The Hate Play* (Box Clever, UK Tour), *Epiphany* (Theatre Is, UK Tour), *A Stroke of Genius* (Pleasance London and Edinburgh), *The First Thing That Ever Ever Happened* (Lyric Hammersmith), *Find Me* (Cockpit Theatre).

Chloe is the 2006 winner of the Michael Northern Bursary award from the Association of Lighting Designers.

Emma Laxton | Sound Designer

Emma is the Associate Sound Designer for The National Theatre's production of *War Horse* and was previously an Associate Artist at the Bush Theatre, as well as Deputy Head of Sound for The Royal Court.

Sound designs include: *The Sacred Flame* (English Touring Theatre), *The Physicists*, *The Recruiting Officer* (Donmar Warehouse), *Lady Windermere's Fan* (Royal Exchange), *Black T-Shirt Collection* (UK Tour and National Theatre), *Lay Down Your Cross* (Hampstead Theatre), *Much Ado About Nothing* (Wyndhams Theatre, West End), *Precious Little Talent* (Trafalgar Studios), *The Whiskey Taster* (Bush Theatre), *Men Should Weep, Shoot/Get Treasure/Repeat* (National Theatre), *My Romantic History* (Sheffield Theatres and Bush Theatre), *Travels With My Aunt* (Northampton Theatre Royal), *My Dad's A Birdman* (Young Vic), *The Gods Are Not To Blame* (Arcola Theatre).

For the Royal Court: *The Heretic*, *Off The Endz!*, *That Face* (and Duke Of York's Theatre, West End), *Gone Too Far!*, *Incomplete and Random Acts of Kindness*, *My Name Is Rachel Corrie* (and Playhouse Theatre; Minetta Lane Theatre, New York; Galway Festival and Edinburgh Festival).

Sue Needleman | Casting Director

Television includes: *The Dumping Ground*, *Old Jack's Boat*, *Get Defenders*, *Young Dracula*, *The Wickedest City*, *Tati's Hotel*, *Getting Out Alive*, *Locked Up Abroad*, *Tracy Beaker Returns*, *The Bill*, *The Revenge Files of Alistair Fury*, *The Giblet Boys*, *The Queen's Nose*, *No Cooks, No Vets, No Gardeners*, *Gypsy Girl*, *The New Adventures of Robin Hood*, *Sunny's Ears*, *Harry II*, *Goggle Eyes*, *Springing Lenin*, *Now That It's Morning*, *Shall We Gather at the River*, *Never the Sinner*, *Out of Order*, *Off to the Wars*, *Outing and Dogplant*, *The Black Rainbow*.

Film Includes: *Blessed*, *Hot Gold*, *Preaching to the Perverted*, *This Boy's Story*, *Say Goodbye*, *Courage Mountain*, *The Paperhouse*, *The American Way*, *Ping Pong*.

Samuel Wood | Assistant Director

Theatre as a director includes: *Laridae, The Rain King, Little Foot, Moments Designed* (West Yorkshire Playhouse),*Casanova Jack, Love me Contender, Miss Brando* (Theatre in the Mill, Bradford), *Killer Joe, 4:48 Psychosis, Spring Awakening, Agamemnon, Bacchus and Pentheus Ovid Tales.*

Theatre as an assistant director includes: *Steptoe & Son* (Kneehigh Theatre), *Where Have I been All My Life* (New Vic Theatre, Newcastle), *King Lear, Jack and the Beanstalk, Angus, You: The Player* (West Yorkshire Playhouse), *Original Bearings* (Slung Low); *The Workroom, The Tyrant* (RADA); *Toad, Sunday Morning at the Centre of the World* (Bad Physics).

Samuel has held the position of Assistant Director for RADA, West Yorkshire Playhouse and Kneehigh Theatre.

Jenny Grand | Stage Manager

Jenny graduated from Guildford School of Acting with a Diploma in Stage Management in 1995. She has worked in theatres all over the UK and has also toured in Europe and the USA.

Companies include: RSC, The Young Vic, Donmar Warehouse and Trafalgar Studios, Complicite, Manchester Royal Exchange, Bristol Old Vic, Lipservice, Theatre Royal York and the Haymarket Theatre, Basingstoke.

Alecky Blythe | Emma

Alecky is a playwright, actor and founder of Recorded Delivery Theatre Company.

She has written and performed in: *Come Out Eli* (Arcola, transferred to BAC), *All the Right People Come Here* (New Wimbledon Studio), *The Day of All The Days* (London Eye/Lift Africa '05 Festival) and *Cruising (*Bush).

Writing for the stage includes: *Strawberry Fields* (Pentabus, National Tour), *I Only Came Here for Six Months* (British Council/ KVS and Les Halles Brussels), *The Girlfriend Experience* (Royal Court and Drum, transferred to Young Vic), *Do We look Like Refugees?!* (National Theatre Studio and British Council/Rustaveli Theatre Georgia and Assembly Rooms), *Where Have I Been All My life?* (New Vic) and *London Road* (National Theatre, Cottesloe and Olivier revival).

Writing for television includes: *A Man in a Box, The Riots: In Their Own Words, The Rioters.*

Awards include: Time Out Award for Best Performance on the Fringe 2004 (*Come Out Eli*), Edinburgh Fringe First Award 2010 (*Do We look Like Refugees?!*), Critics Circle Theatre Award 2011 for Best Musical (*London Road*).

Kellie Bright | Fen Knowles

Theatre includes: *Incomplete and Random Acts of Kindness* (Royal Court), *Paul, Sparkleshark* (National Theatre), *Love and Money* (The Young Vic), *King Lear, The Front Line* (The Globe), *Crawling in the Dark* (Almedia), *A Conversation, Mary Barton, Cold Meat Party, Snake in Fridge, The Seagull, Palace of the End* (Manchester Royal Exchange).

Television includes: *Great Night Out, One Night, Horne and Corden, Hotel Babylon, New Tricks, The Catherine Tate Show, Come Rain or Shine, Rock 'n Chips, Vital Signs, Jericho, Silent Witness, Cor Blimey, Nature Boy, The House That Jack Built, It Must Be Love, The Upper Hand.*

Film includes: *Kinky Boots, Imagine Me and You, Ali G – IndaHouse.*

Radio includes: Kate Aldridge in *The Archers.*

Kellie was nominated for the 2003 Ian Charleson Award

Max Calandrew | Andrezj

Theatre includes: *Daughter in Law* (The Library Theatre Company), *Single Sex, Galka Motalka, 1984* (Manchester Royal Exchange).

Theatre whilst training includes: *Three Sisters, Spidermen, Talk of the City, Les Liaisons Dangereuses, Stags and Hens* and *Great Expecations* (Manchester School of Theatre).

Tim Delap | Edward Knowles

Theatre includes: *Persuasion* (Salisbury Playhouse), *Translations* (Abbey Theatre, Dublin), *The Crash Of Elysium* (Punchdrunk), *Hamlet* (Sheffield Crucible), *The History Boys* (UK Tour/Wyndhams Theatre), *Vincent In Brixton* (Salisbury Playhouse/Tour), *The Old Country* (Trafalgar Studios/Tour), *As You Desire Me* (Playhouse Theatre), *All's Well That Ends Well* (RSC/West End), *Loot* (Theatre Royal York).

Television includes: *Black Mirror 2, Titanic - Blood And Steel, Doctors, Four Seasons, Midsomer Murders, Foyle's War, To The Ends Of The Earth, Silent Witness, It's A Girl Thing, The People Are The Forest.*

Robert Gwilym | Sir Roger Glynn

Recent theatre includes: *Under Milk Wood* (Tobacco Factory), DC Karn in *Sus* (The Bridewell), Cockburn in *The Front Line* (The Globe), *Love The Sinner* (National Theatre), Title role in *Macbeth*, The Sorcerer in *Aladdin*, Creon in *Antigone* (Bristol Old Vic).

Other Theatre includes: Eddie in *A View from the Bridge* (Touring Consortium), *Dancing at Lughnasa* (Abbey Theatre Dublin, West End and Broadway), *Much Ado About Nothing, Ivanov* (Strand), *Julius Caesar* (Exchange), *The Seagull, The White Devil, The Way of the World* (Greenwich),

Behind Heaven (Manchester Royal Exchange), *Cymbeline, Pericles, Baal, The Suicide* (RSC) and more than 25 productions at The Citizen's Theatre, Glasgow.

Television includes: *Ashes to Ashes, The Hutton Enquiry, The Bible, The Bill, Forty Something, Ultimate Force, Casualty, Taggart, Tiger Bay, Chef, Soldier Soldier, Lovejoy, Much Ado About Nothing, Operation Julie, The Brothers Karamazov, South of the Border* and *The Professionals*.

Film includes: *Frankenstein's Army, Mussolini, Sakharov, On the Black Hill.*

Radio includes: *Sense and Sensibility, Guards! Guards!, The Fantasy of Dr Ox, Quantum Man, Three Days that Shook the World, Delayed Departures, A City Full of Swindlers.*

Ben Lee | Jack Tilly

Theatre includes: *Dr. Faustus, King Lear* (The Globe), *Othello* (Sheffield Crucible), and *Coriolanus* (RSC).

Television includes: *The Bill.*

Film includes: *Miss In Her Teens* and *The Humpersnatch Case.*

Claire Lichie | Interviewer/ Jack Lawyer/ Paula

Theatre includes: *Remembering Strawberries* (Nabokov/Southwark Playhouse), *Testing The Echo* (Out of Joint/Birmingham Rep), *Cruising* (The Bush), *Gladiator Games* (Sheffield Crucible/Theatre Royal, Stratford East); *Way To Heaven* (Royal Court), *All The Right People Come Here* (The Bush), *Miss Private View* (Soho), *Lovers* (Gielgud), *The Witch of Edmonton* (Southwark Playhouse), *3Some in Soho* (Soho), *Blue Funk* (Old Red Lion), *Yerma* (London Classic Theatre Company), *Skin* (A.C.T. Theatre Company), *Love's Labour's Lost* (Etcetera), *The Snow Queen* (National Tour), *Twelfth Night* (Cambridge Shakespeare Festival), *Much Ado About Nothing* (Cambridge Shakespeare Festival).

Television includes: *Agony*.

Film includes: *Inbetweeners* (Universal Pictures).

William Mannering | Chris

Theatre includes: *The God of Soho, Dr Faustus, As You Like It, Love's Labours Lost, Midsummer Night's Dream, Romeo and Juliet, We Are The People, In Extremis* and *Antony And Cleopatra* (Globe Theatre), *The Picture* (Salisbury Playhouse), *Vincent River* (Hampstead Theatre), *The Winslow Boy, West End, The Divine Right and The Merchant of Venice* (Birmingham rep)*, Rookery Nook, Present Laughter* and *The Inland Sea* (Oxford Stage Company), *Summer Lightning* (Northampton), *Steven's Last Night In Town* and *Games People Play* (Jacobs Well) and *Midsummer Night's Dream, The Lion, The Witch and The Wardrobe* and *The Winter's Tale* (RSC).

Television includes: *The Jury, Blackhearts in Battersea, Dalziel and Pascoe, Sharpe, Casualty, Holby City, Trial & Retribution, Tchaikovsky, Urban Gothic, The Inspector Lynley Mysteries, Coral Island, The Infinite World of H.G. Wells, Heartbeat, Wuthering Heights, Unfinished Business,* and *The Old Curiosity Shop.*

Film includes: *Master & Commander, Breaking the Code* and *Jackpot.*

Marianne Oldham | Linda Tilly

Theatre includes: *The Real Thing* (WYP/ETT), *Hamlet* (The Factory), *Design for Living* and *Persuasion* (Salisbury Playhouse), *Uncle Vanya* (Belgrade Theatre/ Arcola Theatre), *The Years Between* (Royal and Derngate, Northampton), *The Girl in the Yellow Dress* (Market Theatre, South Africa / Traverse, Edinburgh), *An Inspector Calls* (Novello Theatre/ Wyndhams Theatre), *Mimi and the Stalker* (Theatre 503), *Troilus and Cressida* (Cheek by Jowl), *The Changeling* (English Touring Theatre), *Sweethearts* (Finborough Theatre), *How Many Miles to Basra* (West Yorkshire Playhouse), *The Cherry Orchard* (Southwark Playhouse), *Present Laughter* (Theatre Royal Bath), *Finally the Girl* (The Old Red Lion), *The Gentleman from Olmedo/Venetian Twins* (The Watermill), *We Happy Few* (Malvern Theatre).

Television includes: *Doctors, The World of the Impressionists.*

David Partridge | Henry

Theatre includes: *Barefoot In The Park* (Yvonne Arnaud & Tour), *Twelfth Night* (Original Theatre tour), *See How They Run* (Original Theatre tour) *Stone Cold Murder* (Vienna's English Theatre), *The Sound of Murder* (The Mill), *Charley's Aunt* (Theatre Royal Bath/tour), *A Midsummer Night's Dream* (Open Air, Regents Park), *The Taming of the Shrew* (Open Air, Regents Park), *The Comedy of Errors* (Northcott, Exeter) *The Safari Party* (Library Theatre, Manchester), *The Gentlemen* (Jermyn St. Theatre), *Measure for Measure* (Riverside Studios), Taming of the Shrew (Nottingham Playhouse)

Television includes: *Mrs Biggs, Doctors, The Bill, Holby City, Hotel Babylon, Where the Heart Is, Casualty, The Vice* and 3 series of *A&E.*

Film includes: *Young, High and Dead.*

Elexi Walker | Kim Lopez

Theatre includes: *DNA* (National Tour), *The Taming Of The Shrew* (Southwark Playhouse), *To Kill A Mockingbird* (York Theatre Royal and Touring Consortium), *The Vagina Monologues* (UK Tour), *Desert Boy* (Nitro Theatre), *These Four Streets* (Birmingham Rep).

Television and Radio includes: *Doctors, Reality Check.*

The Producers

Ben Rix

Ben Rix runs Rix Productions and is the head of drama at BAFTA award winning Little Brother Productions, where he produces original drama for television, film and radio with the brightest emerging writing talent in the UK.

Mimi Poskitt

Mimi Poskett is the Artistic Director of Look Left Look Right, a documentary theatre company based in the East of England. The company creates work that examines how people are affected by big moments in national and international news. The creative process is defined by the use of verbatim text combined with a site-specific setting. LLLR has won two Fringe First Awards (2008 *The Caravan* and 2011 *You Once Said Yes*). LLLR's most recent production, *NOLA*, a verbatim play about the Macondo Oil well disaster of 2010, premiered at the Edinburgh Fringe 2012. Mimi has also worked for The Guardian, ITV and the BBC. In 2007, she won a Royal Television Society award for a documentary about 9/11.

The Producers would like to thank the following individuals and organisations, without whose assistance this production of *You Can Still Make a Killing* would not have been possible:

Leah Archer	Adam Povey
Joanne Benjamin	James Rigby
Jolyon Coy	Brian Rix
Anthony Doran	Nina Scholar
Paul Elliott	Tom Skipp
Philippa Grand	Ros Terry
Margaret Grand	Dave Williams
Tarek Iskander	English Touring Theatre
Nathaniel Jessel	National Theatre Studio
Grant Jones	Regent's Park Open Air Theatre
Jonathan Keeley	The Young Vic
Matt Noddings	

Southwark Playhouse Staff List

Southwark Playhouse

'Southwark Playhouse's brand is as quirky as it is classy'
The Stage

Southwark Playhouse Theatre Company was founded in 1993 by Juliet Alderdice, Tom Wilson and Mehmet Ergen. They identified the need for a high quality accessible theatre which would provide opportunities for the best emerging companies and practitioners, and also act as a major resource for the local community. They leased a disused workshop in a then comparatively neglected part of Southwark and turned it into a flexible theatre space.

The theatre quickly put down strong roots in Southwark, developing an innovative, free at source, education programme. It has worked closely with teachers, Southwark Borough Council, businesses and government agencies to improve educational achievement and raise aspirations. This programme is in great demand and attracts substantial funding each year.

Over the past fifteen years the theatre has established itself as one of London's leading studio theatres, representing high quality work by new and emerging theatre practitioners.

In 2007 it moved to its current premises in vaults beneath Platform 1 of London Bridge Station where it is home to a 150-seat studio theatre and a brand new secondary performance space, The Vault, which now serves as a platform for developing and nurturing cutting edge theatre.

Under successive talented artistic directors, Mehmet Ergen (now Artistic Director of the Arcola Theatre), Erica Whyman (now Artistic Director of the Northern Stage Company), Thea Sharrock (recently directed *After the Dance* at the National Theatre and *Cause Célèbre* at the Old Vic), Gareth Machin (now Artistic Director of Salisbury Playhouse) and Ellie Jones, Southwark Playhouse has become an indispensable part of theatre in London.

2011 marked the start of Chris Smyrnios' tenure as Artistic Director and an exciting programme of work that included Philip Ridley's first world premiere in three years, *Tender Napalm*, a major revival of Hannah Cowley's *The Belle's Stratagem* and the critically acclaimed *Parade* and *Bound*, both of which received five star reviews in the *Evening Standard*. The year culminated with Southwark Playhouse being the recipient of the Peter Brook Empty Space Award 2011 with Fiona Mountford praising the 'high-energy, life-giving spirit' of the theatre.

2012 is Southwark Playhouse's last year in its current home before it relocates to temporary premises to make way for the redevelopment of London Bridge Station.

For more information about our forthcoming season and to book tickets visit www.southwarkplayhouse.co.uk. You can also support us online by joining our Facebook and Twitter pages.

You Can Still Make a Killing

Take, have and keep are pleasant words.

Medieval saying

Business is the art of extracting money from another man's pocket without resorting to violence.

Max Amsterdam

Acknowledgements

I would like to thank Ben Rix and Mimi Poskitt for their support and for their tireless work as producers.

Many thanks to the entire cast and crew for their tremendous energy and commitment.

I am grateful to the Peggy Ramsay Foundation for financial support during the writing process, and to the National Theatre Studio for hosting a workshop and reading for the play. I am also grateful to Michael Sommer, Gert Pfafferodt, Tarek Iskander and Nathan Curry for their help.

Most of all I would like the thank Matthew Dunster for his many insights and his encouragement.

Characters
in order of appearance

Edward Knowles, *mid-thirties*
Jack Tilly, *mid-thirties*
Fen Knowles, *mid-thirties*
Linda Tilly, *mid-thirties*
Sir Roger Glynn, *fifties*
Emma, *over forty*
Interviewer, *over thirty-five*
Kim Lopez, *twenty-seven*
Andrzej, *twenties*
Henry, *over forty*
Chris, *thirties*
Jack's Lawyer, *over thirty-five*
Paula, *over thirty-five*

A slash in the dialogue (/) indicates that the next actor should start their line, creating overlapping speech.

Act One

Scene One

Conference room.

Edward *and* **Jack** *sit across from each other.*

While they are both in full-on City suits, **Edward** *wears a rather odd purple-plaid shirt.*

Jack *throws some documents on to the table.*

Jack   This is MBS fodder.

Edward   That's why the haircut's so deep –

Jack   'Deep'? With re-hypothecation / it's –

Edward   Through an SPV – nice, investment grade, paying a fantastic coupon.

Jack   Yeah SOP.

Edward   Keep that haircut at forty per cent – free money for you.

Jack   Why's / that?

Edward   Look at it. People will be drooling.

Jack   If the first big thing I'm bringing to the fund is something –

Edward   This good? Just to make things clear – in terms of bottom line: our firms have all the GMRA and ISDA docs.

Jack   Yep.

Edward   We've done business with your fund in the past –

Jack   Yep.

Edward   When you traded here at the bank, you and I made a lot of money together.

Jack   True that.

Edward   This is a good idea.

No response.

Edward   I'm just trying to sell you this as a gift, a fucking present – celebrate your ascendancy to that swishy fund –

Jack   It could fall by fifty per cent.

Edward   *No* –

Jack   How about this – I take this on and then I want to get out because I look like a proper fist to my new boss, because I've taken a punt on a pile of shit from 'my old bank'? It'll take at least two weeks to wrap this stuff up in the BVI and then we've got to get it CRA-ed then market the stuff – honestly, I'm starting to think even a fifty per cent haircut isn't deep enough, as much as I want to do business with you and be a party to you, NFW.

Edward   You want to do something else? You got alternatives, enlighten me. What great ideas are sweeping that fancy hedge fund of yours?

Jack   Now I . . .

Edward   Go on, throw me a bone – what are you guys looking / at?

Jack   I don't have any tips, okay? Haven't been there long, you know –

Edward   This is a really good thing – someone else is going to make a kill –

Jack   No, it's not – look, I'm a simple man. Yes we have bilateral agreements between First Brook and this place: basis swaps, CDS, repo, fx, collateral switches, you have already sold us good stuff. But maybe the fund has got enough exposure to this bank right now –

Edward *shakes his head.*

Jack   Maybe we're looking tapped / out

Edward   Yeah yeah okay but you *worked* here.

Jack   And the share price hasn't come back. I cashed in all my stock options at a bloody discount –

Edward   Cry me a river, all right? It's a share price, it goes up and down for *all* of us. The point is you worked with *me*. You know how things move around here, you see this for what it is – a good thing –

Jack   Not at that haircut.

Edward   You got to take it –

Jack   Why? Because I've gone on to something bigger and better, does that fucking obligate me / to –

Edward   No no, and there's nothing wrong –

Jack   Of course not it's a great bank I loved it here but I can't help feeling this little piece of shit – (*He holds up the documents.*) is actually about some resentment, some fucking resentment that I moved on.

Beat.

Edward   It's a great product.

Beat.

Edward   And I'm delighted for you.

Jack   It's all right but not at that haircut.

Edward *checks his watch.*

Edward   Yeah, uh . . . fine, all right: I'll give you fifty per cent but you got to be all / in.

Jack   Fifty per cent ?

Edward   Yeah.

Jack   Fuck off.

Edward   Deal?

Jack   At fifty per cent ?

Edward   Why not . . . congratulations.

Jack   Is there something I'm missing here?

Edward   Yeah, I'm trying to make you money.

Jack *looks over the documents.*

Jack   Can you wrap it quickly?

Edward   Like a present.

Jack   Done.

Edward   I'll get it all over to you.

They stand up as **Edward** *gathers all the documents.*

Edward   You enjoying it over there at least?

Jack   Loving / it.

Edward   How's it working for Sir Roger anyway?

Jack   He's all right. Walks around with a hard-on eighteen hours a day thinking about himself.

Edward (*laughs*)   How often does he interrupt you?

Jack   I don't speak. I just listen. Fine but his PA I mean, that bitch makes like eighty-five a year just to walk around with her arse in the air condescending people on his behalf –

Edward   Hey he's outsourcing, very efficient.

He checks his watch again.

Jack   Fuck it – I'm all the way out here, let's grab some lunch at Roka –

Edward   Now?

Jack   How often do we see each other any more?

Edward   I got other stuff.

Jack   It won't cost you nothin'.

Edward   Really?

Jack (*smiles*)   I'm a client now. The bank pays.

Edward   But . . .

Jack   But what?

Edward (*checks watch*)   I need to scoot and ah . . . go and buy some stuff.

Jack   Buy 'stuff'? Fucking traders do that for / you –

Edward   No I need to like go and *buy* something.

Jack   Like shopping?

Edward   Yeah.

Jack   Maxi-pads for your weak vagina?

Edward   Yeah right –

Jack   What object is so important in Canary fucking Wharf that we can't go and eat?

Beat.

You got a woman here now.

Edward   No –

Jack   You're going off for a little sneaky bang-bang – who? Megan in PR? Couldn't blame you –

Edward   No –

Jack   I hear she fucks like a fat girl –

Edward   It's shirts, all right? I need to go and buy some shirts.

Jack   Yeah . . .

Beat.

Jack   Okay.

Beat.

What's wrong with the one you got on?

He takes another look at **Edward***'s shirt.*

Jack   So you need a new shirt. Do it some other time –

Edward *takes a large glossy voucher out of his pocket and throws it on the table towards* **Jack***, who picks it up.*

Edward   It's this voucher. Ends today.

Jack   You're blowing me out for a shirt voucher?

Edward   Twenty-five per cent off.

Jack   Never mind damaging our new business relationship. I could have had half a row of *California Maki* stuck down my throat by now thank you, thank you –

Edward   I thought you'd understand because uh . . .

Jack   What?

Edward   Because . . . it's kind of magic to me.

Beat.

It's kind of like a magic voucher.

Jack   You've gone over to the other side. You're deranged –

Edward   No I mean it, it started . . . at uni – one day it just appeared in my pigeonhole. Every pigeonhole had one, a voucher, 'sixty per cent off' –

Jack   Not bad.

Edward   I got my stuff, came to London in the full kit. I was feeling it. And then I fucking crushed the interview here. I was in.

Pause.

Edward   Don't you remember when that happened for you?

Jack   Yeah of course – actually I don't remember last week, I'm sure it was great but I play life forward: I'm hungry. Now –

Edward   Every time they send me one of these things, I still use it. Maybe I don't need to but it's like . . . knocking on wood you know? Or seeing two magpies or –

Jack   I really am hungry –

Edward   I've got to do it, it's like tradition . . . and when I walk around wearing these shirts I always think you know, 'I bought this with a voucher' and I'm ready to take on the world. Everything feels . . . aligned.

Pause.

You know what I mean?

Jack   No one knows the thrill of being cheap like I do, I think in a previous life I was a Scot with no arms.

Edward   And now –

Jack   We have all this!

He motions around them.

Both of us! . . . Even Croydon boy.

Beat.

Edward   'North Surrey' is my preferred place of origin . . . motherfucker. And I live in Fulham now.

Jack   Yes you do, yes you do so there's nothing to be jealous about . . . you fucking freak.

Edward   What can I say, when you didn't return my calls I was worried you'd forgotten about me.

Jack *starts packing up.*

Jack   We just had our summer holiday.

Edward   With the new baby?

Jack *nods.*

Edward   Congratulations again by the way –

Jack   Thanks . . . And we *are* the first in the group to have three.

Edward   Does it really matter which one of us has three /
first?

Jack   Certainly seems to for the missus – didn't you ever
want a third?

Edward   Nah, I don't think so; so where'd you go anyway?

Jack   CUBA.

Edward   Wow – good?

Jack   *Great.* Snorkelled, the boys learned to play baseball.

Edward   Brilliant sport.

Jack *shows* **Edward** *a photo on his BlackBerry.*

Jack   The people there are so poor, they make baseballs out
of rubber bands.

Edward   Amazing . . . I love stuff like that.

They finish packing up. Only the voucher is left on the table. **Jack** *picks
up the voucher to hand it to* **Edward**.

Jack   Cubans must be the most entrepreneurial people in the
world. They have to be. Otherwise they'd die . . . It's a
wonderful place.

Just before he hands it to **Edward**, **Jack** *takes a second look at the
voucher and then tears it to pieces.*

Jack   But we're not Cubans.

He throws the shreds back on to the table. **Edward** *looks at them: he is
not best pleased.*

Jack   So *I'm* going to buy you lunch at Roka, and then *I'll*
buy you some shirts myself this weekend God damn it, you're
such a useless sack of shit.

Edward *looks up at* **Jack**. *They both break into laughter.*

Edward   If you say so big man.

They leave. The shreds of the voucher remain on the table.

Scene Two

Living room.

Fen *and* **Linda** *resting in the reclined 'side-plank' position for yogalates, with top hand on their hips.*

Even though they are wearing yoga kit and are lying on mats, at first they look like they are just regally lounging around.

A few feet behind them is one of those giant, posh prams.

Soft, transcendental music plays.

Linda   Last time.

Both women lift themselves into side-plank pose. Then they bring their top knee and top elbow together five times. **Linda** *is moving more quickly than* **Fen***, who starts to struggle.*

Linda *shifts into the 'single-kneeling balance' position. She's effortless, while* **Fen** *now drags.* **Linda** *is able to wrap around and grab her ankle with her hand.* **Fen** *sticks to the more basic pose.*

Linda   Focus on your core. That is the most important.

She switches sides. **Fen** *follows, barely.*

Linda   And . . .

They both go to kneeling.

Well done!

Fen   Yeah . . .

Linda *hops up, full of energy, and checks the pram.*

Fen   I can't believe you're the one who's just had a baby.

Linda   I really want to get back into it, I'm so thankful for your help.

Fen   Yes, well, I'm enjoying it. I'd love to lose my *own* baby weight . . . ten years on.

Linda   It's a habit, that's all. 'We are what we repeatedly do.'

Beat.

Fen   Yes.

Linda (*looking into pram*)   Arms are the hardest.

Fen   Should I turn off the music?

Linda   No, I think it helps her sleep.

They roll up their mats. In time . . .

Fen   You're the first to have three.

Linda   Funny that, isn't it?

Beat.

Fen   How's it feel, any different?

Linda   Scary: there are more children than parents. The boys are running a bit wild, now that we have to take an eye off them sometimes.

Fen   That sounds difficult.

Linda   It's okay. It's nice.

The baby, Violet, cries. **Linda** *rocks the pram to quiet her.*

Linda   Then there's *moments* with her.

Fen   How nice to do that again.

Linda   Here.

She lets **Fen** *rock the pram.* **Fen** *loves it, and admires Violet.*

Linda   How are yours?

Fen   I caught Harry putting Kathy's chinchilla into the dryer. He said it was a science experiment for school.

Linda   Oh God.

Fen   I know – nobody ever says 'I want to have a *teenager*'. But before you know it –

Linda   Harry's not a teenager.

Fen   Twelve is close enough, trust me. Edward and I feel like we're really living on the edge.

She admires Violet.

I miss this stage.

Linda *smiles, then checks her watch.*

Linda   I'm sorry I'll have to dash before too long; I've got tea with the hedge-fund wives later –

Fen (*impressed*)   Wow. Already?

Linda   Yes, I know. Mother's never been so happy about Jack. She never really forgave him after he quit medicine, but that's finally . . . better.

Fen   What's Sir Roger like?

Linda   Jack says he's 'very hedge fund'.

Fen   And what's that?

Linda   Expects massive compensation for being slightly better than average . . . Jack is loving that part.

Fen   And the wives?

Linda   A bit brusque . . . The *museums* their husbands fund – and they don't even know art; they ask their wives what shows to put on.

Fen   That sounds fun.

Linda   It's brutal – I meet these women, they're all pushing to do the next big Picasso exhibition before anyone else, or the next Monet – they all want to sponsor some super-famous painter just so they can look good and . . . they've got the power. You ought to come meet them sometime – but we better brush up on our art!

Fen   Absolutely.

They both suddenly make ghastly faces.

Linda   Oh sorry. I think we have a situation.

Linda *doesn't know where to go to change Violet.*

Fen   Change her in the kitchen and I'll make some coffee before you go.

Linda   Great.

Fen's *hip gives a bit as she walks, causing obvious pain.*

Linda   Oh dear, you sore? Do a couple salutations, help you cool down.

Linda *and Violet exit to kitchen.*

Fen *does a salutation: shaky at first, but with growing confidence.*

In time, **Edward** *enters behind her. She doesn't hear him come in.*

He wears a business suit, and carries a stylish document case. His tie is loose and he looks completely dishevelled. He wears a bright, stylish shirt.

He stands and watches **Fen** *do her salutation for a bit, and then:*

Edward   Hi.

Fen   Oh – hi darling. What time is it?

Edward (*checking his watch*)   Two o'clock. Almost two o'clock.

Fen   What are you doing home?

Edward   Uh . . .

Fen   Have you taken the afternoon off?

Edward   Yeah.

Fen   Aren't you feeling well?

Edward   What the fuck are you doing?

Fen   Yogalates.

No response. She grabs the fat on her upper arm.

You don't want me to get elephant arms, do you?

No response.

What's wrong?

Fen *goes to touch* **Edward**'s *forehead, he recoils.*

Edward   I'm fine I'm not ill.

Fen   You're scaring me.

No response.

Are you drunk?

Edward   It's fine it's fine. It's / fine –

Fen   Did you have a big lunch or –

Edward   Eating is cheating.

Fen   How long have you been drinking?

Edward *shrugs, unsettling* **Fen**.

Fen   Something's wrong. Shall I sit down?

Edward *sits down.*

Edward   Sure. Thanks.

Fen   How bad is it?

Edward   Very. End-of-the-world bad.

Fen   It's not – (*As in 'It's not that bad'.*)

Edward   I lost my job.

Fen   You lost your job.

Edward   Yeah – not literally, as in . . . Lehman's filed.

Fen   'Filed'?

Beat.

Filed what? Filed a complaint against you?

Edward   Filed as in 'filed for bankruptcy'.

Fen   Jesus . . . ahhh –

Edward   HOWEVER, however look – let's all just put it in perspective – the bottom line is is that . . . I think there are . . .

it's not the end of the world, you know, people lose their jobs and I'm pretty good at what I do so . . . we just got to put it in perspective / okay?

Fen   'Bankruptcy'?

Edward   Yes.

Fen   *How?*

Edward   Everyone twisting our / bollocks.

Fen   I thought you were going to get taken over, you said last / night –

Edward   They bailed. It came back to Barclays and they *wanted* to buy us but . . .

Fen   But what?

Edward   The government blocked it! Can you believe that? It was a corporate . . . *euthanisation* –

Fen   I don't . . . so what does it mean for you?

Edward   I'm toast, that's what it –

Fen   I mean what's going to happen to *you* – your stock?

Edward *notices the pram, and leaps towards it anxiously.*

Edward   What the fuck is that?!?

Fen   Linda's here.

Edward   *Linda?*

Fen   The *shares* Edward –

Linda *enters with Violet.* **Edward** *immediately pulls it together and peacocks. He seems calm and sober.*

Linda   Edward, hello.

Edward   Hi.

Linda   Gosh, it's . . . Monday.

Edward   Yeah I forgot some documents, so –

Linda   Oh.

Edward   And this must be Violet. Hello, Violet?

Edward *peeks in to say hi to Violet.* **Linda** *picks up his breath.*

Linda   Drinking on the job?

Edward   It was lunch and I realised . . .

Linda   Jack says Lehman's probably getting taken over –

Edward   Busy time.

Linda   Things are so volatile, aren't they?

Edward   Violet is so beautiful.

Linda   Jack keeps saying how great all the volatility is, makes it easier for traders to make money on the upswings, is that true at the bank too?

Pause.

Edward   Yes.

Linda *checks her watch.*

Linda   I'd better go anyway.

She puts Violet down into the pram.

Linda   Oh my God I left her poopy nappy in the kitchen!

She heads to the kitchen.

Fen   It's fine, I'll –

Linda   No no I couldn't *bear* it.

She exits, embarrassed. **Fen** *is dumbfounded.*

Fen   What the fuck are you doing?

Edward   DON'T LET HER KNOW. We can't let them . . . *know* we can't let them *see* –

Fen   If Lehman's gone down she's going to know in like *minutes* –

Edward   Fine by then I'll have something else and then it will be fine, like nothing's –

Fen   What about the stock?

Linda *enters with a Tesco bag holding the nappy.*

Linda   I stole a Tesco bag.

Fen   You can leave it here.

Linda   No I'll deal with the poopy nappy.

She gives air kisses to **Edward***.*

Best of luck. I'm sorry about Lehman I hope a nice bank takes it over, like Barclays? And, you know, you're all right.

Edward *nods.*

Linda (*to* **Fen**)   I'll ring you later. I need someone to talk about art with!

Fen   Of course.

Linda *leaves.*

Fen *looks through the curtain to check that* **Linda** *is really gone.*

Edward *sits back down on the sofa.*

Fen *turns and looks at him expectantly, but gets nothing.*

Fen   Edward. Tell me you got the –

Edward   If a company doesn't exist, you can't really own stock in it. My shares are gone.

Fen   Surely that's not . . .

Pause.

All of them?

Edward *nods.*

Fen   But they couldn't . . .

No response.

Fen   We were supposed to sell them. I told / you –

Edward   You / can't –

Fen   We could have bought the *house* with them –

Edward   We *did*, okay? My shares were the collateral on the fucking mortgage.

Fen   We didn't need one! How could you −

Edward   Because then you get the shares *and* the house, the value of both going up and . . . there's not a choice anyway: selling your stock options is a massive sign of . . . weakness. People would have known. A personal choice like that to hurt the bank and . . . it's all over for you.

Pause.

Fen   So what are you saying?

Edward   I'm saying ninety per cent of my wealth portfolio was in Lehman shares I never sold. It was just a good, old-fashioned fucking.

Fen   . . . Then where do we stand?

Edward   About three million in debt and no assets.

It's finally sinking in for **Fen**. *She starts to get tearful.*

Edward   I'm not the only one you know, it's happened to lots of people.

Fen   Is that supposed to make me feel better or something?

Beat.

Edward   Yes?

Pause.

Fen   Can't anyone help you? Who can help − what about Charlie? What about *Jack*, Jesus what about *Jack* he's working at that big fund can't he get you a / job?

Edward   Oh my God. I sold Jack a pile of shit, an absolute bag of shit.

A dazed pause. **Fen** *sinks into her seat.*

Edward   But it wasn't my fault.

The soft, transcendental music still plays.

Scene Three

Sir Roger's *office, First Brook Capital hedge fund.*

Jack *sits and stares into space.*

Sir Roger *stands. He holds a speech, and sometimes refers to it, as he rehearses.*

Sir Roger 'While we've lost a third of our value, the future looks promising as we . . . '

Beat.

Bright. (He corrects his speech.) 'The future looks *bright* as we dump the dogs and keep the racehorses. Things may be expensive but they're still cheap. Our liquidity will put First Brook Capital in perfect position to grasp green shoots of recovery as this crisis recedes.'

Beat.

Jack *(waking up from his trance)*   Yeah! Brilliant.

Sir Roger   Do you think that plays on a conference call?

Jack   Absolutely –

Sir Roger *(cold)*   Thank you for your expert opinion.

Jack   It'll be / fine –

Sir Roger's *mobile phone rings. He checks the caller ID.*

Sir Roger   Fuck. It's George – he better have my bastard collateral . . . but if he's ringing me direct . . .

He is already out of the door.

Jack *doesn't know what to do. He picks up* **Sir Roger**'s *speech and walks around pretentiously while mouthing the words.*

Jack   'Things may be expensive but they're still cheap.' That's brilliant.

Emma, **Sir Roger**'s *PA, walks in behind him and observes.*

She carries a glass of iced tea and some forms. She places the iced tea on the table.

Emma   Has your meeting finished?

Jack *replaces the speech on the table.*

Jack   *Yes* . . . Probably, actually. Yes.

Emma   Then I'm sure you appreciate . . .

She hands him a form.

Jack   What, a P45?

Beat.

You want me to fire someone?

Emma   I don't know what Sir Roger told you but . . . What did Sir Roger tell you?

Beat.

Emma   You're a very bright guy. I'm sure you'll get picked up somewhere else.

Jack   You're letting me go?

Emma (*patronising*)   Afraid so, efficiencies and . . . everything. There's just one little detail –

She hands him another form. He doesn't take it.

Our non-disclosure agreement. It's a condition for your severance package. I need you to sign this so I can process things smoothly –

Jack   I don't need these.

Emma *laughs. Then a pause, which bores her.*

Emma   Can I just tell you how untidy your workspace is? Can you please tidy it before you leave, cleaning up after you is not part of my job description and it will help me process your severance much more quickly.

Jack *still does not take the form. She puts it on the table and leaves in a patronising way.*

Jack *puts his form on the table and sinks into a chair, dazed.*

Sir Roger *enters.*

Sir Roger   FLN Tech is gone. They've evaporated. George has fucked it. They're off the map.

Pause.

How do I keep investors on board without pulling in collateral obligations? It's not fair, I'm not fucking responsible let someone else bleed their bullshit why – Where's my damn speech?

He goes to the table and grabs the non-disclosure agreement and P45 by mistake.

Sir Roger   I feel like I'm rewriting this fucking thing every twenty minutes.

He looks at what he's holding and realises.

Sir Roger   Did Emma come in here already?

Jack *nods.*

Sir Roger   I was getting to that. (*Indicating his speech.*) It's an acute situation. But at least we have our health and families, right? We are not eighteen-year-old squaddies in Afghanistan –

Jack   What are you talking about? I can make you money right now. You know this isn't necessarily an intelligent decision on your behalf – you're just reacting emotionally.

Sir Roger*'s eyebrow rises at this disrespect.*

He takes a couple of packets of sweetener from his inside coat pocket. He empties them into his iced tea.

Then he takes a very expensive pen out of his coat and stirs the iced tea with it.

Sir Roger (*while stirring*)   I am trimming operating costs. Investors need to see that.

He replaces the pen in his coat.

Take a nice six-month holiday. By then things will be better, funds will be hiring and you'll be in an outstanding position rela/tive –

Jack I don't want a holiday – it's a time of stress that creates opportunities –

Sir Roger Spare me the business school cant.

Jack I'll show you how I can / make –

Sir Roger I'm not interested in your delusions of grand –

Jack Just give me one month and I'll / show –

Sir Roger (*laughing*) Counterparties are going down! We've done deals with them, paid out our money to them and they no longer exist. How do you think our balance sheet is going to look when *that* dust finally clears? So you're out, you're gone. And I'm sure you'll be very successful.

Jack Then I –

Sir Roger You're going out into the wilderness and you're not coming back . . . *capisce?*

Jack Then I won't sign your non-disclosure. I'll go out there and someone else will hire me right now. I'm a smart guy and I know everything your fund is doing to manage the crisis.

Sir Roger You can't defect like that.

Jack I don't need your severance.

Sir Roger I opened the kimono to you, generously. I expect reciprocal trust.

Jack *shrugs.*

Sir Roger If you take our strategies somewhere else that would technically breach your contract, even without signing the NDA.

Jack Yeah and who's going to prove that?

Sir Roger   We won't need to – the lawyers will bury you in paperwork.

Jack   And I'll take you to the cleaners for wrongful dismissal.

Pause.

I just want a chance. Give me a month.

Sir Roger   Listen –

Jack   I'm not going to be that little *piñata* everyone's kicking the crap out of, so if you can signal that forward pathway, great.

Pause.

Sir Roger   I'll give you another month if you sign this non-disclosure. Right now.

Beat. **Jack** *signs.*

Sir Roger   You're a prize shit, you know that?

Jack   I'm glad we're finally starting to understand each other.

Sir Roger *heads for the door.*

Sir Roger   Lots of luck.

Jack   It'll be fine.

Sir Roger   No it won't. Nothing's working any more.

Jack   Everyone's just paranoid, it's killing companies. The best part of the collapse: tons of companies going bankrupt. That's what's going to help me. A dark time all round, perfect. Everyone else is too scared to make sense of it.

Scene Four

Bank.

Edward *sits across from the* **Interviewer***, who is looking at his CV.*

Edward I have vast experience in SPVs, SPEs, hybrid-protected notes, series three mezzanine participatory issues, high-yield bonds, multi-layered deferred compensation plans and Cayman-based self-funding high-grade senior-protected debt-absorbing multi-entity notes.

Interviewer Your mezzanine experience . . . did you ever come across cross-tier disputes between debt syndicates?

Edward Frequently and persuaded potential litigants that their distinctions were optimal.

Interviewer How sensitive were the rollovers to interest rates?

Beat.

Edward Very.

The **Interviewer** *scrutinises* **Edward***'s CV.*

Interviewer You're married.

Edward Yes.

Interviewer You married young?

Edward Yes.

Interviewer You must be very happy.

The **Interviewer** *scrutinises* **Edward***'s CV.*

Interviewer What is your sense of the future with regard to the self-financing re-hypothecation structures domiciled within reliable tax havens?

Edward I believe what will be witnessed over the coming months and years is that Section 15c regulation will be given much more teeth, thereby compromising current structures, which in turn will require significant amendments, potential mass redemptions and serious restructuring in order to maintain funding requirements and subscriber bases.

Interviewer   Hmm . . . What do you think of our building?

Edward   It's very nice.

Interviewer   And the dry cleaner downstairs sells cigarettes. Thank God.

Edward   Yes.

Interviewer   Things will get better, I'm sure. We'll come out of this on top.

Edward   Of course.

Interviewer   And I'm quite interested in your ability to structure index-linked floating rate derivatives that hold a strong correlation with our current product suite.

Edward   Yes . . . yes.

Pause.

Interviewer   Yes what?

Edward   Of course. I would probably umm – structure them . . . with ones that hold the strongest correlations.

Interviewer   I'm asking: how would you do it?

Edward   I'd probably . . . identify the underlying ahhh – yes: I don't think I've ever *technically* done that, but in theory it's a small leap.

Interviewer   A small leap? A *small leap* – you think a floating rate instrument is easy to manoeuvre in a new product suite? Don't you know what happened to Harbour Tree Capital in the last quarter of '07? Blew up in an instant.

Pause.

Christ, I arranged an interview because I thought you were a bona-fide expert in structuring index-linked floating rate derivatives in matching suites. Is that not true? I thought you might be able to provide serious distribution opportunities to clients who hold most of this family of products. You can't?

Scene Five

Empty room in the new extension, **Edward** *and* **Fen***'s house.*

Edward *sits cross-legged on the floor. There is an open newspaper in front of him.*

He holds a tin can to his ear, which is connected to a string that runs offstage (the kind of crude telephone kids make for fun). **Edward** *listens to the can and speaks into it.*

Edward   Un.

Beat.

Deux.

Beat.

Trois . . . Quatre . . .

Fen *enters: she has followed the string to find out where he is. She carries a hoover.*

Edward   Cinq . . . Six . . .

Fen   What are you doing out here?

Edward   Admiring our new extension –

Fen   In French?

Edward   – while helping Harry with his homework, in French. You done?

Fen   Not quite.

Edward *(into his tin can)*   Harry: go hoover the bedrooms for your mum.

He listens, but there's no response.

Little bastard . . .

He drops the can.

Hung up on me.

Fen *(indicating open newspaper)*   Who's hiring?

Edward   Nobody.

Fen   You need to get out there and network darling.

Edward   It'll happen, don't worry. For now I've got some quality time with the kids –

Fen   Harry got into another fight at school.

Edward   You're joking – he didn't tell me that.

He picks up the tin can.

Fen   He's bigger than the other kids. He gets pushed into these things.

Edward   Because he's bigger than the other kids?

Fen   Actually, I think it comes from you.

Edward   Me?

Fen   Well . . . you're from Croydon. It's probably genetic.

Beat. **Fen** *feels bad for what she said, so gives* **Edward** *a kiss on his head.*

Fen   But you're still cute . . . Have we decided on his school trip to France?

Edward   I don't have a job.

Fen   But if we're frugal – I think Harry should go. He needs something to expand his horizons, get him out of his sulking –

Edward   You're going to send him to France to stop sulking?

Fen   Maybe it will inspire him, tap into his inner Ernest Hemingway, he needs to be *interested* in something so he'll . . . behave. We'll just spend less around here –

Edward   Yeah yeah all right let's send him, who knows, maybe France will civilise him.

Fen makes to leave, but **Edward** *doesn't move.*

Fen   Come downstairs and help him with his homework in person.

Edward   Is Kathy still watching *Pretty in Pink*?

Fen   Probably . . .

Edward   Then I'll stay out here.

Fen   Okay babe . . . I'll be so glad when the extension is finally done.

Edward   Yeah – I was thinking that Kathy could move into this room, and Harry could have the room downstairs, and then we could have a bit more peace around the love nest.

Fen   Okay.

Edward   Stop sharing the walls with our children.

Fen   But now that we have extra rooms around the 'love nest' . . .

Beat.

We could have another baby.

Beat.

I want another baby. I always did. I always said I wanted three.

Edward   We settled on two.

Fen   No we didn't.

Edward   I don't have a job.

Fen   I know but . . .

Edward   But what?

Fen   It takes nine months to have a baby, by then things will be all right . . . You'll find something.

He keeps a poker face. She doesn't give an inch.

Edward   I'm trying.

Fen   But what about . . . outside of finance, something else.

Edward   Like what?

Fen   Insurance or just a *company*. Go work for a company. You've got a track record –

Edward   In finance.

Fen   Of being bright –

Edward   You want me to become a civilian?

Fen   If it will get us going. If it will let us have another child.

Edward   WHAT DO YOU WANT FROM ME? ARE WE NOT . . . We've got to be *careful* with this –

Fen   Things will get better.

Edward   We've got to be *careful*, all right? It's –

Fen   Things will be better and now's the time –

Edward   What if they don't? And we have another child?

Fen   We'll manage.

Edward   We'll . . . Forget it.

Fen   You can't / forget –

Edward   Look at what's happening! And every night I wake up it's the same God damn thought: 'I don't want them growing up like I did'.

Fen *laughs, unkindly.*

Fen   You say it like it was so . . . Croydon was hardly –

Edward   No, NO, it wasn't – we're not talking poverty, all right? It's just . . . a place. You *end up* there . . . asking your mum for cinema money then loathing the cinema because you saw her digging through her handbag to scrape three-fifty together and you know she's just trying to make it to Friday . . . Going around with her every Sunday night delivering those fucking shirts she ironed for single blokes, 40p a pop, the way they'd treat her at the door –

Fen   She didn't do that for ever –

Edward   When Dad was out of work, would you do that for me now?

Beat.

Fen   There are worse things.

Edward   Like hell you would, but you'll say something like 'A hundred years ago people would have been thrilled to have a job ironing shirts' yeah true very clever but . . . they didn't have it right next to them – the new cars and money – home counties filling up with all sorts of stuff and holidays . . . maybe that was all just a mirage, and it's just gonna be a select few in the end who get all that good stuff – the public schools, the travelling, the opportunities, *fine* – BUT MY KIDS ARE GOING TO BE PART OF THAT FEW . . . They're not going to be left sitting around at home staring at each other –

Fen   We won't –

Edward   And the quickest way to get like that is to have too many kids and no job, fucking trust me on that, all right? So just let me get something where I can work my bollocks off for . . . *THIS* . . . I can't do anything else. It's too late to become a surgeon, sorry.

Weird, unintelligible sounds echo faintly through the room. **Edward** *realises they are coming from the tin can. He picks it up.*

Edward (*into can, sharply*)   Will you leave us alone? Mummy and Daddy are talking.

He slams the can down.

Fen *goes to* **Edward** *and wraps her arms around his head, holds him for some time.*

Fen   Hey we'll figure it out . . . right?

Edward *leans up and kisses her.*

Fen   Why don't you try . . . the Starbucks. Fulham Road.

Edward   That's not really going to change the momentum –

Fen   Not to *work* there you idiot – you go there, you meet . . .
I don't know . . . Mary Cawkwell.

Edward   Uh-huh.

Fen   Her husband works at a good fund.

Edward *nods.*

Fen   She's there all the time with her friends. You casually go
up to her. 'How are you? How's your husband? How's the
business?'

Edward   Right. You know . . . that's actually an idea.

Fen   Get some access.

Edward   Yeah . . . Okay . . . Okay.

She kisses him.

Fen   'Fulham. Starbucks. World domination.'

She laughs.

Blackout.

In the darkness, echoing sounds of Harry speaking French through a tin-can phone.

Scene Six

Starbucks.

Edward *sits in a Starbucks-style chair across from* **Linda***, who is also
in a Starbucks-style chair. Beside her is a pram.* **Edward** *is dressed in a
City suit. They drink coffee out of Starbucks mugs.*

On the table between them are **Edward***'s laptop, phone,* Financial
Times *and his five empty coffee mugs. On* **Linda***'s side of the table is a
stack of large, glossy art books. She is looking through one of them while
rocking the pram with one hand.*

Linda   Fen has persuaded me: Violet will need a horse. We'll need to buy at the right time. Your daughter's horse is still so little, *sweet* – girls like to buy a little horse and *plan* don't they? So they can see a future together.

Edward   Umm . . . yeah.

Linda   Some girls I know even stay home from family holidays to take care of their horse. Are you going to let Kathy do that?

Edward *shrugs.*

Linda   But how did you even find the right one? It must be like finding a soulmate . . . who's actually a horse.

Edward   Talk to Fen. When we bought Kathy's there was one that I really liked – strong legs, always in front of the others, beautiful really – but then Fen gave it a closer look and said, 'He has stupid eyes. He won't be able to see the fence to jump over it.'

Linda   Gosh.

Edward *sees someone and waves as the person walks by.*

Edward (*to the person*)   Hello.

Linda (*remembering*)   George Stubbs.

She grabs a book and rifles through it.

Horses were his favourite subject.

Edward   Never heard of him.

Linda   Of course you haven't, you've spent your whole life in an office that's why I'm *educating* you. Look . . .

She holds up a horse painting.

Edward   Yeah – Do you know when I can get in touch with Jack? I can't seem to –

Linda (*browsing mindlessly through the book*)   He's just always busy with work.

Edward   How's he doing?

Linda   Fuck knows. Whenever I ever ask him something like that he always says 'Great' in a really serious way. When other people ask how he's doing he always says – (*Quite serious and mysterious.*) 'We're good'.

She goes back to her book.

Edward   Will he be around tonight?

Linda (*re: book*)   There's a serious message in all this.

She indicates the stack of art books, then looks around so as not to be heard as she speaks to **Edward** *conspiratorially.*

Linda   It's like the hedge-fund wives only know Van Gogh, Picasso, Monet and Damien Hirst, those are the only shows they want to sponsor – can you imagine that we get the same big exhibitions every year because these women hardly know anyone else, and their husbands will do whatever they say?

Edward   Maybe they just like the best; you can't blame them for liking the best –

Linda   Who says they're 'the best'? People need to judge for themselves – we need to give the 'sponsors' some education. Otherwise it's monkey-see-monkey-do.

Edward   Great but people are still going to like Picasso.

Linda   Who, 'the public'? The public doesn't know good from bad, and for the *museums* to be led by people who don't know anything about art is just fucking madness.

She shuts the book and stands up.

Linda   So wish me luck. I'm meeting someone now who thinks pronouncing it FUN KHOKH (*i.e. the Dutch pronunciation: f- as in fit, -u as in bun, kh- as in Scottish loch*) makes her some sort of connoisseur. She also thinks that Henri Gaudier-Brzeska is a blood disease.

Edward *hands her some business cards.*

Edward   Take some cards, if you meet anyone who might be looking for someone. And please ask Jack if he's heard of anything. I haven't talked to him in ages.

Linda   He's just busy. I haven't seen him so little since he was doing twenty-hour shifts in the hospital – remember that?

Edward   Vaguely. I always knew he'd come over to finance.

Linda *inspects one of* **Edward**'s *cards as* **Kim**, *a young African-American woman in a power suit, enters with a laptop bag and a mug of coffee.*

She looks around for a place to sit, then stands against the wall, sipping her mug and reading the Financial Times.

Linda (*re: his card*)   It looks funny.

Edward   There's no company on it.

Linda   Oh of course, sorry. I'll give some to Jack too.

Edward   Tell him I'm looking quite hard.

Linda   And *you* give my best to Fen – things will get better.

Edward   We'll be fine.

Linda (*affectionate but also patronising*)   You'll be fine, you'll be fine.

She leaves.

Kim *immediately rushes to her vacated seat and sits down. She is now talking on her mobile, but it's like she's struggling to hear. She sets up her laptop while on the phone. She is obviously American.*

Kim   A hundred thousand euros. Take everything else, put it in roubles. Roubles – *roubles.* Just *do it* and call me when the finger's out please.

She hangs up, gives a frustrated sigh then becomes lost on her laptop. **Edward** *takes an interest, looks at* **Kim** *while sipping his coffee. Their eyes meet.*

Kim   Do you mind if I work here?

Edward   'Work'? Be my guest.

She glances behind them.

Kim   I didn't think Starbucks was going to be so full of prams.

Edward   You're on the Fulham Road.

Kim   Doesn't mean their children should just run all over the place.

Edward   What do you expect? They're mostly Americans.

They laugh.

Edward   Who you buying roubles for?

Kim   Me.

Edward   Day trading?

Kim   Something like that.

Edward *fingers his* Financial Times.

Edward   Check out the dollar. It hasn't been this oversold since May '08.

Kim   Umm . . . *okay*. You're into trading?

Edward   I was at Lehman.

Kim *suddenly stops, puts her mobile down. She gives* **Edward** *her full attention.*

Kim   Wow, like, you looking? Headhunters?

Edward   They've gone the way of British cars. (*He holds up his* Financial Times.) How about you? Are you from the City?

Kim   I'm kind of freelancing. Thought I might work here but I can't hear myself think. How do you *stand* it?

Edward   Look at the clientele.

Kim   Mothers?

Edward   Wives.

Kim *takes a good look at the clientele, realises what* **Edward** *is saying.*

Kim   How is that working for you?

Edward   Who knows. I got a couple leads, maybe an interview?

Kim   You don't sound very happy about it.

Edward   I'm not here to be happy. I'm here to make my wife happy. She thinks this will work so for now I just . . . play along.

Kim   Why?

Beat.

Edward   You're not married, are you?

Kim *shakes her head.*

Edward   To be fair I can't really think of anything better right now.

Kim   Maybe you just need to try somewhere else – Café Nero?

Edward   Too studenty.

Kim   You should go to the gym.

Edward   Everyone's busy grunting. If you stay too long you look desperate.

Kim   A pub would be better than this.

Edward   I'll be seen as a drunk. But if I drink coffee and read newspapers all day, somehow that's all right. And I've found that enough caffeine helps me forget about my mortgage.

Kim   I just want to *work* here, you know? 'Work'?

Edward   Then go to Café Nero. It has an upstairs.

Kim   . . .

Edward   You can't get a *pram* upstairs. On the upper floor you can have your . . .

Kim   'Coffice'.

Edward   Whatever.

Kim's *text message sound goes off, she reads it.*

She stands and packs up.

She looks around at all the wives, then at **Edward**.

Kim   You really come here every day?

Edward   I've got a house, two kids – what are you, twenty-three, twenty-four?

Kim   Twenty-seven.

Edward   That's not too old. You can afford to just wait this out.

Kim   I never said I was made redundant. I quit two weeks ago.

Edward   You *quit*?

Kim   Yeah.

Edward   '*Quit*'?

Kim   I quit.

Edward   *Why?*

Kim   Things I want to do.

Edward   Where did you work?

Kim   Green Forest. / The private equity –

Edward   The private equity group? They hiring?

Kim   I don't know.

Edward   You look a bit young for someone from private equity.

Kim   It was the next logical step . . .

Edward   From where?

Kim   Goldman Sachs.

Edward *is shocked.*

Edward   You were at Goldman? You're a baby, look at yourself, you're a little foetus. Your father works there?

Kim   No.

Edward   Oh my God . . .

Kim   I *am* twenty-seven.

Edward   You 'quit'? What was your . . .

Kim   In-house M&A – Merchant Banking division.

Edward   Any of those firms still exist?

Kim   You were at Lehman.

Edward   I sold products that made people money, not just flipping companies for quick cash / or –

Kim   And business is taking off, thankfully.

Edward   . . . Is it?

Kim   Yeah. Too bad you structured-products guys are probably extinct –

Edward   I wouldn't say we're 'extinct'.

Kim   It's about *real* businesses now – the ones about to go under, thousands of them. You can get them cheap if you have some money. Everyone else is too scared to take them on, it's perfect.

Edward   . . .

Kim   You ought to hurry up and get into the game. Everyone's panicking. Everyone's scared. In a climate like this, you can still make a killing.

Pause. **Edward** *suddenly shuffles through his papers.*

Edward   I ought to give you my CV. I can *sell* and understand complex . . .

Kim   I'm good thanks. If you get really desperate try the Financial Regulations Authority. I hear they're hiring.

Edward *smiles with a strained confidence.*

In the background, **Andrzej** *comes in and begins mopping the floor.*

Kim   I'm serious. It's a great outpost for people on 'gardening leave', then you come back to the private sector with some contacts for 'effective negotiating'.

Edward   I'll work here as a barista before I work for the FRA.

Kim   Hey they're hiring –

Edward   I'm just not built that way, all right?

Kim   It's a job tip for you – and I'm not even lactating.

Edward *leers at* **Kim** *as she departs.*

Kim   Thanks for the advice – Café Nero!

She exits. **Edward** *sinks into his seat in an angry panic.*

He slowly picks up his Financial Times, *but is unable to read it. He puts his head back in frustration.*

Andrzej *still mops.*

Fen *enters. She holds car keys in her hand.*

Fen   Hiya.

Edward   You missed Linda.

Fen *looks around for her.*

Fen   Do you still want to come with me to pick up Kathy?

No response.

Don't leave me to the pony club mothers on my own.

Edward   Can I at least drive?

Fen   If you like.

Edward   I do. I've had twelve cups of coffee today and my reflexes are really peaking.

He starts to pack up. **Fen** *sees the mugs on the table.*

Fen   Those are all yours?

Edward *nods while packing up.*

Fen   I thought we talked about not spending so much money /
here.

Edward   You're right, it's just . . .

Fen   What?

Edward   It's a coffee shop, what do you want me to do?

Fen   Don't get despondent, you found that interview for
Friday.

Edward   They rang, said the position was no longer viable.

Fen   No longer 'viable'?

Edward   Which means someone else had a friend and got
there first. Fortunately I could drown my sorrows in a
frappachino.

Fen *frowns.*

Edward   It's just coffee. It's / just *coffee.*

Fen   That's not how you felt about money when you were
working. That's not what they taught you at Lehman. I'm right
and you know it.

Edward   Of course you are.

Fen   You'll find something.

I'm trying.

Fen   Then keep trying and stop wasting your money. You're
a *banker.*

They go to exit and walk past the mopping **Andrzej**. **Edward** *slips a
little. Then he pauses. He turns around, angry.*

Edward   I slipped.

No response.

Did you hear me? I slipped.

Andrzej *takes a concealed iPod earphone out of his ear.*

Andrzej   Huh?

Edward   I said I almost slipped and broke my neck because of your mop – your mopping – aren't you supposed to wait until Starbucks is closed before you do this? So that your paying customers don't fall over and break their necks?

No response.

I'm talking to you? You don't care . . . You're just doing it now so you can go home early.

No response.

This is the problem – this is the problem – you can't even mop, you're supposed to wait until we're all gone but you're more important than your own customers. And I almost get my neck broken because of it – because you're not doing your job properly! You're asleep at the wheel!

Beat.

Andrzej *places a* 'DANGER: WET SURFACE' *sign right next to* **Edward**, *then continues mopping.*

Scene Seven

Conference room, First Brook Capital.

Smart new shirts sit neatly folded on the table. There are two blue shirts, two yellow and two pink. Each pair is identical, just slightly different sizes.

A few boxes of cuff links are also laid out.

There are price tags on each object, and corresponding receipts next to them.

As he speaks, **Sir Roger** *takes off his coat and shirt, then tries on one of the pink shirts.* **Emma** *watches attentively. There is a landline phone on the table.*

Sir Roger   If you don't have a competitive advantage, don't compete. The second oldest law of the jungle after 'anything goes'. The lions don't have to worry about either rule, they're too busy fucking between buffet dinners. The second oldest law is for zebras, anteaters, iguanas, *rats.* Let them worry, spend their time freaking out, getting desperate, taking crazy risks to survive – I'm able to focus calmly on the future, I'm focused on managing disaster, it's one of my strengths . . . so I'm going to enjoy this moment, optimistic / that –

Speakerphone Voice   Roger, can you hold on just a second?

Sir Roger   Sure.

A dull techno music is heard.

Sir Roger *has finished trying on the new shirt. It is way too tight. He looks like an idiot.*

Emma   Looks like we underestimated the cookie monster's appetite.

She unwraps the bigger pink shirt.

Speakerphone Voice   Roger?

Sir Roger   Yes.

Speakerphone Voice   We decided to begin processing our redemption.

Sir Roger   How much?

Speakerphone Voice   All of it.

Sir Roger   Don't be a panic seller, William –

Speakerphone Voice   Our decision is final.

Sir Roger   One more quarter and –

Speakerphone Voice   We'll get the paperwork going right away.

Sir Roger   William, we go back further than I care to admit.

Speakerphone Voice   And it's always a pleasure, Roger.

A dial tone. **Sir Roger** *presses the button to hang up.*

Emma   Was that bad?

Sir Roger   A big chunk of change, walking right out the door.

He's taken off the smaller pink shirt and throws it on his office chair.

Sir Roger   We're going to win this bloody game…

He walks into the larger pink shirt, which Emma holds out for him.

Go update the termination papers for those fuckers we're –

Emma   They were updated last night.

Sir Roger   Really?

Emma *nods.*

Sir Roger   . . . And there's something else: I booked holiday flights for my family –

Emma   You can do that all on your own?

Sir Roger   Of course I can! You just follow the sodding . . . screens.

Emma   I'm very impressed.

Sir Roger   It's just . . . my daughter. She got married last summer and I forgot about her surname. That it's changed. So now I've booked her bloody ticket . . .

Emma   With the wrong surname.

Sir Roger   Yes. It could cause problems with security.

Emma *laughs, and goes to his desk to fold up the pink shirt. She packs it into a Thomas Pink bag.*

Emma   'Security'? It will cause problems with your daughter more like it. And your wife.

Sir Roger *gives her a dirty look, but she is not intimidated.*

Emma   Consider it sorted.

Sir Roger   Thank you –

Emma   But please do *me* a favour: the next time you ask me to help you fire someone like that Jack Tilly – don't take them back.

Sir Roger   Yes yes you've said, you've made yourself more than clear thank you very much.

He looks through the various little cuff-link boxes.

Sir Roger   *Now* . . . little sailboats I like these – little strawberries? Are you mad?

Emma (*sulking*)   For the Global Berry Congress.

He starts trying them on.

Sir Roger   Ah! Excellent idea.

He looks at all the things he has on.

Emma   You look very nice in that.

Sir Roger   Thank you.

Emma   But I'm still waiting for an apology.

Pause.

Sir Roger *takes off his shirt so he is bare-chested.* **Emma** *still glares at him.*

Pause.

Sir Roger   I'm sorry about Jack.

Emma   You gave him a month, it's been three.

Sir Roger   I won't do that to you again.

Emma   Yes you will.

Sir Roger *peacocks:*

Sir Roger   I do value you as −

Jack *comes in and interrupts. He sees the bare-chested* **Sir Roger** *with* **Emma**.

Jack   Sorry −

Sir Roger   What is it?

Jack   Do you have a moment?

He gives **Emma** *a disapproving once-over.*

Sir Roger   If you're quick.

Jack   One sec.

Jack *leaves.*

Emma   Get rid of him please? He's such a prat.

Sir Roger   Maybe so but for now . . . he's saving us. He's actually making money.

He tries on a pink shirt.

I go into these meetings and everyone's looking at him for answers. They're looking at me with a fucking . . . question mark.

Emma   You're slipping?

Sir Roger *is fully dressed in the pink shirt.*

Sir Roger   Not funny. I've got to keep my arms around the business, otherwise . . .

Emma   What?

Sir Roger   You become like one of those lobsters they put in warm water and gradually boil. You don't realise what's going on until it's too late.

Jack *comes in. He hands some documents to* **Sir Roger**, *who flips through them.*

Sir Roger   You see the football this weekend?

Jack (*indicating reports*)   Too busy. Missed it.

Sir Roger   Chelsea played Sunderland. Who do you think won?

Jack   Sunderland. Chelsea's form has been really bad recently.

Sir Roger   That's right. Amazing, you took the underdog.

Jack   Yeah I guess.

Sir Roger   Like in some of these deals.

Jack   No, no, I've done the research – my notes should explain everything clearly.

Sir Roger   I'm glad it's clear.

Jack   I think –

Sir Roger   I wouldn't want it to be over my head.

Jack   Of course not.

Sir Roger   But that stock purchase you made last Tuesday . . .

Jack   Yes?

Sir Roger   That company was in awful shape – why didn't you get my permission before the purchase?

Jack   Mmm . . . what's the point? By the time you woke up it would have been too late.

Pause.

Didn't it pay off?

Beat.

What I'm saying is –

Sir Roger   Yes?

Jack (*indicating reports*)   For this one, I don't want to buy stock. I want to buy the whole company.

Sir Roger *tries to hand the file back to* **Jack**.

Sir Roger   So give it to my private equity guys. You know the drill.

Jack *does not take the file.*

Jack   But I'm the one who found it.

Sir Roger   So what?

Jack   This is what I've always wanted to do.

Sir Roger   Who cares?

Jack   I'm not going to lose what I've found. It's not fair.

Sir Roger   'Fair'?

Jack   So if I can't do it, I don't think anyone else will. The secret will get out of the box.

Pause. **Jack** *takes the file from* **Sir Roger**.

Sir Roger   Stay here and shut up for one second.

He marches into the private room adjoining his office.

Emma *stares at* **Jack**. *It starts to bother him:*

Jack   Just tell him to buzz me when –

Emma   You did see the football, didn't you? You knew Sunderland won.

Silence. **Jack** *gives* **Emma** *a look that says 'Yeah I did, and you can fuck off'.*

Sir Roger *marches back into the room from the other door. He has a fresh shirt, tie and jacket on. He also carries two glasses of whisky. He is peacocking, fully ready for battle.*

Sir Roger   Emma: sort my daughter's ticket please.

Emma   Are you / sure –

Sir Roger   NOW.

Emma *leaves.*

Sir Roger   Remind me what I did to deserve you.

Jack   You're not going to try to fire me again, are you?

Sir Roger   I just think there are some fundamental misunderstandings –

Jack   Because you can't. You'd lose too much in the next quarter.

Beat. **Sir Roger** *hands a glass of whisky to* **Jack**.

Sir Roger   'Pride cometh . . . '

Jack   And this is the best job I've ever had. Cheers.

He chinks **Sir Roger***'s glass cheerfully.* **Sir Roger** *is less enthusiastic.*

Sir Roger   Better than medicine?

Jack   Absolutely.

Sir Roger   That was a rather brave jump, don't you think?

Jack   Not really.

Sir Roger   Didn't you like cardiology? There are some people who wish you'd go back to it.

Jack   I just thought it was kind of a dead end.

Sir Roger   Really?

Jack   Once I saw all this, I couldn't see any real alternative.

Sir Roger   Fair enough . . . But didn't any aspect of it appeal?

Jack   Hmm . . . I've got a photo at home of me surrounded by kids at the hospital; I assisted in valve operations for all of them.

Sir Roger   'Assisted'?

Jack   It's still on my wall.

Sir Roger   I have a hard time imagining you 'assisting' anyone.

Jack   I was just a student then.

Sir Roger   Did you ever get to do it yourself?

Jack   I did a lot in the lab, operating on stray dogs. We'd even try heart transplants on them, the ambitious stuff. One time we were bored and had two dogs left, so I transplanted the head of one dog on to the other. A two-headed dog. It lived for eight minutes.

Sir Roger   Jesus Christ, why would you do that?

Jack   See if it worked.

Sir Roger   You're a sick bastard . . .

Emma *enters but* **Sir Roger** *doesn't notice: he's measuring* **Jack** *up.*

Sir Roger   If you want to buy that company, go ahead. Do it . . . why the hell not?

Beat. **Jack** *nods 'thank you' and leaves.*

Emma *looks horrified, and approaches* **Sir Roger**. *He sees her coming.*

Sir Roger   Not a fucking word, all right? Just leave it.

Pause.

What?

Emma   He really reminds me of you, just a lot younger.

Scene Eight

Lights up on a closed door. **Edward** *and* **Fen** *sit in front of it.*

Fen   Please COME OUT! *Please,* Harry . . .

She knocks on the door.

Edward   Harry, you're upsetting your mother now.

No response.

Come on.

Edward *knocks on the door.*

Fen   HARRY!

Edward   It was just a fight. Boys get in fights.

Fen   It wasn't just a fight.

Edward   I mean he's *twelve*.

Fen   He stuck a pencil into someone's tongue.

Edward   They punished him enough, didn't they? Banning him from his trip.

Fen   There will be other school trips.

Edward   Yeah but this is the big one to France, remember? 'Ernest Hemingway'?

Fen   They said he's violent!

Edward   So was fucking Hemingway!

Fen (*to Hal*)   JUST BE THANKFUL THAT YOU *GO* TO THAT SCHOOL, WILL YOU?

No response.

He does awful things then likes to feel sorry for himself, can't you / see –

Edward *checks his watch and stands up.*

Edward   This is kind of cutting into my Starbucks time. I hate to leave but . . .

Fen   Can't you wait?

Edward   That Starbucks has become a very competitive marketplace. I've been seeing other people there, bankers I know. There's not enough seats.

Fen   Really?

Edward   I've still got some leads . . . and you'd be proud of me. I only buy one cup of coffee a day now. Sometimes I don't buy any.

Fen   Good for you. HARRY DO YOU KNOW WHAT YOUR FATHER –

Edward *kisses* **Fen**.

Edward   He'll be fine.

Fen   They said he's even started bullying girls.

Edward   He probably just wants their attention.

Fen'*s mobile rings offstage. She exits to go answer it.*

Edward *sighs and lingers, then knocks on the door softly.*

Edward   Mate, you all right? . . . It's tough but that's the way it is, you don't always get what you want, France is nice but mostly it's just . . . weird . . . Someday you'll go someplace that . . . bizarre . . . probably . . .

Harry?

It happens – look at me, I'm . . . outside . . . but I just got to stick it out, until I get another chance . . . to *compete*, get back in the game, it'll happen for both of us don't worry yeah?

He lapses into silence. He doesn't know what to say.

He begins to walk away from the door and head to Starbucks.

The door unlocks and opens a couple of inches, but no one can be seen behind it.

Edward *turns and looks.*

Edward   Hey, mate.

Fen *comes rushing in.*

The door snaps shut.

Fen   EDWARD, God . . .

Edward   What?

Fen   It's Millie –

Edward   Millie?

Fen   Millie's gone – someone's taken Millie.

Edward   Oh shit. Where's Kathy?

Fen   She's out there. She's hysterical. (*Into her mobile.*) I'll ring you back. *Stay there.*

She hangs up and then begins to dial.

Edward   What are you doing?

Fen   Calling the police –

Edward   Why?

Fen   Someone stole our horse, I've got to –

He grabs the phone from her hand and hangs it up.

Edward   Tell me what happened.

Fen   She went out to go riding with the Crosheres and Millie's just . . . gone.

Edward   Oh no.

Fen   Someone took her – maybe someone else –

Edward   I'll handle it.

Fen   You? What are you going to do?

No response.

Well?

Edward   Well what?

Fen   You don't seem terribly concerned.

Edward   I'm really concerned. Calm down.

Fen   Calm *down*?

Edward   And we'll . . . Everything will be fine.

Fen   Ed/ward.

Edward   I'll take care of it.

Fen   Do you realise how much her horse is *worth*?

Edward   About forty-eight and a half grand.

Fen   Probably . . .

Pause.

How do you know that?

Edward *shrugs.*

Edward   I sold Millie.

Fen   Sold her?

Edward   I didn't think Kathy was going out today –

Fen   You absolute tosser.

Edward   *I* bought it. It was my horse too.

Fen   How could you not tell me?

Beat.

Edward   I knew this would be a difficult conversation.

Fen   So you let this happen.

Edward   I had to do –

Fen   You've broken her heart! How could you not fucking tell me?

Edward   I couldn't tell you because –

Fen   What the hell is wrong with you?

Edward   – you'd ask questions. I'd have to . . .

Fen   What?

Edward   Tell you that the house is next.

Fen *laughs. Her laughter is somewhere between derisive and scared.*

Fen   No, that's not going to happen.

Edward   Yeah it is.

Fen   *Borrow*, borrow until you / get –

Edward   Fen.

Fen   Just make the next payment.

Edward   I know, I know I've looked at it from a thousand ang/les –

Fen   Sort it out.

Edward   I can't.

Fen   If you want to sell that horse for glue then fine, you said we wouldn't have to move that's the one thing you promised me. We made a compromise, *two* children and the house.

Edward *shrugs.*

Fen   I'm not . . . I've personalised this house – I'm not leaving now.

Edward   It's nice –

Fen   'Nice'? We had a skip outside for eight months – the extension, the garden –

Edward   You can have a garden in a new house.

Fen   *The lane.* Both your children walk up that lane every day. It's such a nice . . . short cut . . .

Edward   You can personalise a new house –

Fen   You can't personalise a lane. It's just there.

No response.

It's how they get to school so make the fucking payment! If you have to borrow more to do it then borrow more to do it –

Edward   No. My Lehman shares were collateral on the mortgage and they're long gone, so the bank wants £300,000 back right away. It's like a margin call. I've got twenty-eight days. I'm not going to make it. Not even close.

Pause.

Fen   Well then, I'll / speak –

Edward   And I've already talked to your father. He said he might be able to get us 30K in the short term – even offered to sell his car . . . It was a personal . . . low point. He never liked me. He always resented my success.

Fen   You *what?*

Edward   And it's not nearly enough.

Fen   We can't move.

Edward *goes, turning around at the last second:*

Edward   And I told your dad to keep his car.

He leaves.

Fen *starts to cry. She suddenly bangs fiercely on Harry's door.*

Fen   WHAT'S WRONG WITH YOU WHY CAN'T YOU BE A NORMAL BOY?

Scene Nine

Starbucks.

Edward *talking to* **Linda** *at Starbucks. Violet's pram is next to* **Linda***; she rocks it gently with one arm while looking at an art book.*

Edward *looks a bit of a wreck.*

Linda *drinks out of a Starbucks mug.* **Edward** *has no coffee. The table between them is empty.*

Edward   I could cry. I haven't cried in like ten years, and that was only because I got drunk and watched *Kes* right after my dad died. What grates is looking back to where it all started – all the people I was better than, all the others that dropped by the side, left to go other places, packed it in, went travelling and never came back. I fought on and that's what it felt like.

Linda *isn't really listening. She checks on Violet.*

Linda (*in a sweet voice*)   Hello there . . .

Edward   Maybe it's what most people's lives feel like – a fight – but I'm the sum of my experiences; a year ago they were worth something, today . . . fuck all. I have no bid.

Linda *holds up the art book so* **Edward** *can see a picture: Malevich's 'Black Square'.*

Linda   People just know Rothko – 'Rothko this, Rothko that, Rothko slashed his wrists blah blah blah' but Malevich was doing the same thing twenty-five years before. No one knows.

She goes back to her book. **Edward** *is still in his own world, he doesn't really register what she said.*

Edward   The shares. I know it was stupid to have all that money in one place, but they just kept giving you them. No point leaving, no other offer could tempt you away . . . But it's funny; your net worth decimates, and I immediately go into some kind of survival mode –

Linda *holds up 'Black Square' again.*

Linda (*re: book*)   This was a protest against totalitarianism.

Edward   Limit the outflows, things will get better and when they do I'll be bid again – that experience is worth tens of millions in the right environment . . .

Linda   Fucking Stalin.

Edward   At the right time . . .

Andrzej *appears behind* **Edward** *again: this time without the mop or earphones. Instead he just stares at* **Edward**.

Edward   I can sell . . .

Andrzej *taps* **Edward** *on the shoulder.*

Andrzej   You've got to leave the premises. Immediately.

Edward   What?

Andrzej   You have to go.

Edward   Me?

Andrzej   Right away please now.

Edward   What are you talking about?

Andrzej   You haven't bought coffee. You've been sitting here for hours and not bought one.

Edward   You're joking.

Andrzej *shakes his head.*

Edward   That's an outrageous request.

Andrzej   We're business, not a charity –

Edward   I'm *here* for coffee.

Andrzej   No. That wrong.

Linda   *I'll* buy him a coffee, all right?

Edward   The baristas were busy when I came in.

Andrzej   No.

Edward   I'll happily get a coffee now if you're going to –

Andrzej   Stop karade please.

Edward   What?

Andrzej   This karade.

Linda   I think he's saying 'charade'.

Edward (*to* **Andrzej**)   What the hell do you mean by that?

Andrzej   I mean you were warned last week for sitting here whole day and never buying something. And you were warned. Official.

Edward *stands up.*

Edward   *Stupid* – I'll buy your coffee, all right?

Andrzej   Abusing employees with the verbal will not be tolerated.

Linda   Oh you're being ridiculous, please just let / him –

Andrzej   *No.* (*To* **Edward**.) You're banned. This place busy, many people all day and our seats for customers.

Linda   I'll make a complaint about you –

Andrzej (*to* **Edward**)   You go or I ringing security.

Edward   What is this?

Linda (*to* **Andrzej**)   You ought to be ashamed of yourself.

Andrzej   We get many homeless people come here sit with buying nothing. We use company to move them.

Linda *looks around, afraid of being noticed.*

Edward   But I –

Andrzej   Six seconds I ring.

He walks away.

Edward *is frozen with anger and shame, but eventually turns back to* **Linda**.

Linda   You'd better go, you'll get in trouble.

Pause.

Edward   Yeah, okay . . . Bye.

Edward *leaves.*

Scene Ten

The Financial Regulations Authority.

Henry *and* **Chris** *sit across from* **Edward**, *looking over his CV. A bag of nuts sits on the table next to* **Chris**.

Henry   Welcome to the Financial Regulations Authority. I'm Henry and this is Chris. Let me say right away how impressed we are with your application.

Edward   Thank you.

Chris   Yeah you're exactly the hundredth candidate from Lehman Brothers we've seen in the past eight months.

Edward   Wow.

Chris   Amazing. You win a prize. Have a bag of nuts.

He pushes the nuts towards **Edward***, not in a friendly way.*

Edward   I just hope I'm the *best* candidate.

Chris   What's that suit, Gieves & Hawkes or Ozwald Boateng?

Edward (*undented*)   Can't you tell?

Chris   No. I'm an M&S man, and if you come and work here you'll be one as well.

Edward   They make very fine suits.

Chris *picks up the bag of nuts, opens them, and starts eating.*

Henry   How familiar are you with what the FRA does?

Edward   I'm very familiar with what the FRA does.

Henry   Well?

Edward   You regulate financial services markets in the UK and take action against firms that –

Chris   You can read a website. What else?

Edward   You regulate. Things are actually changing now. I can / help.

Chris   How exactly? We don't make the rules here, we certainly don't try to find a way around them, we 'enforce' them – and we don't want refugees.

Edward   I'm not a refugee.

Chris *looks over* **Edward***'s CV.*

Chris   You look it.

No response.

Chris   You look like you've been cutting corners around us for the last ten years –

Edward   I've never broken any law.

Chris   You never walked any fine lines of fraud we should know about?

Edward   No, I was just –

Chris   'Ambitious'?

Beat.

Sorry I've already heard this four times this week from rich blokes down on their luck . . . Now they want to work in the Enforcement Division? Wouldn't you rather be out there, discovering new ways to screw over the public?

Edward (*to* **Henry**)   Is this really neces/sary?

Chris   That tone might work when you're selling crappy products to some delirious fool –

Edward   I never did that kind of thing.

Henry   You know . . . all the Lehman people say that.

Edward   I've never broken any law –

Henry   No, no, sure, it was obviously a function of . . . deep technical knowledge. And Enforcement needs people from deep inside these institutions. You'd have to bring all your knowledge to the table.

Edward   I want to help any way I can.

Henry   Lord Taylor's just made his public call for new regulation and we know City firms will be resisting that, despite how much they've suffered.

Edward   Yes.

Henry   And with three hundred of us monitoring hundreds of thousands of infringers . . . someone like you could be quite useful . . . for about a year, at least.

Edward   Then what?

Chris   Your friends in the City will need someone who's been at the FRA for a while and has good connections here – another reason I'm sceptical of converts.

Edward   I believe in the FRA.

Chris *laughs derisively, while still looking over* **Edward***'s CV.*

Edward   It's clear that the whole thing was caused by a brutal lack of regulation. Any banker will tell you that, at least in private, and I want to help fix the problem, to help bring *law and order* to –

Chris   Slow down mate, I don't want to wake up pregnant.

Henry   So you wouldn't be interested in re-entering the private sector ?

Edward   I want to work for the Financial Regulations Authority. Because it's the right thing to do right now.

Chris   Sure it is . . .

He sees something on the CV and suddenly grows curious.

You're from Croydon?

Edward *nods.*

Henry (*ignoring* **Chris**)   Primarily, the job requires you to find patterns in complex data –

Chris   I'm from Purley.

Edward   Condolences.

Chris   Public school?

Edward   Selsdon High.

Chris   How did someone from a comp in Croydon get to Cambridge?

Edward   I wanted it. It was a lot of work but . . .

Chris *ignores him, still looking at CV.*

Chris   Your 2.2 is less than stellar, how did you get into Lehman?

Edward   It was in Economics.

Chris *is unimpressed.*

Edward   And I played football. Not great for Croydon maybe, but I played for Cambridge.

Chris   You got a blue.

Edward   Two blues. But not many people play football there so −

Chris   Yeah it's all rugby and rowing.

Pause. **Edward** *nods.*

Chris   But the City likes people with blues − we saw a guy in here the other day with a Cambridge blue in skiing. On what fucking mountain? But he had one, and it's good to trade on whatever you can, isn't it? Especially when you're from Croydon . . . or maybe despite it.

Pause.

Who are you?

Edward   I'm someone who . . . really wants to work for the FRA. I want to join the public sector and −

Chris   What did your dad do?

Edward   Sold cars for a while, then he worked in wholesale.

Chris   Selling what?

Edward   Shoes . . . in Surrey and Sussex.

Chris   Like Jimmy Choos?

Edward   No, not like Jimmy Choos.

Beat.

Henry   May we continue the interview?

Chris *tosses* **Edward***'s CV down on the table.*

Chris   I'm satisfied. This guy's got a third-rate degree from a first-rate university. He'll make a perfect civil servant.

Edward   What about the other ninety-nine people you've interviewed from Lehman?

Henry   Some of them now work here, some of them didn't fit the FRA, some of them *fit* but tried to negotiate their salary. We don't negotiate. For this post it's 44 a year, take it or leave it.

Edward   Is there a bonus structure?

Henry   £200 every September plus a WH Smith voucher.

Beat.

Edward   I really do believe in this job, you know.

Henry   We'll take that into account when we decide, thank you.

Chris   Tell me again why we should believe you.

Edward   I just sold my house. I had to.

Chris   And whose fault is that?

Henry   I think he was just saying it was *our fault. (Suddenly a bit threatening.)* Is that what you were saying?

Edward   No I wasn't saying that, I mean the whole crash was clearly . . .

Pause.

Edward   America's fault.

Scene Eleven

Kitchen.

We hear a concert version of Bob Dylan's 'It's Alright Ma (I'm Only Bleeding)'.

Jack, *quite drunk, enters his darkened house. He wears an iPod and sings along to the tune as he pours a drink for himself.*

Linda *enters in her night clothes, unseen, and watches.*

She switches the light on.

Linda   What are you doing?

Jack (*loudly, due to headphones*)   Listening to Dylan, it's a concert version –

Linda   It's late – you're going to wake the baby.

Jack *takes his iPod off.*

Jack   I've been celebrating.

Linda   Celebrating? That sounds innocent enough.

Jack   Yeah. Although we were celebrating in a nudie bar.

Linda   I know. I was being ironic. It's a Tuesday night.

Jack   But I did it again!

Linda   I think I hear Violet.

They look upwards and listen. Silence. Then:

Jack (*whispering*)   I can make noise whenever I want to because I'm the fucking man. *Leg–end.*

She makes to leave.

Linda   I just hope the clients had as good a time as you did.

Jack   I didn't go with clients.

This surprises **Linda**. *She stops and turns.*

Linda   You went to a nudie bar without clients?

Jack   Correct!

Linda   *Why?* To entertain . . . *yourself?*

Jack   'Celebrating'.

Linda   So get a cake.

Jack   Relax – you know women like that only make me think of you.

Linda   . . .

Jack   I mean it in a devoted kind of way?

Linda   Good night.

Jack   Guys at the fund asked me, I couldn't say no.

Linda   Why not?

Jack   Because they were the private equity guys, and they were celebrating *me*.

Linda   Another deal.

Jack   Nine deals in a month. *Nine* – you know who else was doing deals out there? We were the only happy people in the club, the others were . . .

Linda   Staring at the tits of a stranger.

Jack   But in kind of a depressed way, because they've all got such brilliant futures behind them. Not me: I only move on to bigger and better things. Which is why I want to talk to you about the house.

Linda   What about it?

Jack   Shouldn't we expand it? Build a new room?

Linda   I'd just like a *quiet* house / please –

Jack   I've been able to ink agreements that are going to make *so* much money for First Brook.

Linda   Good. I'm proud of you darling.

Jack   *Finally* – she says it.

Linda   I hope you had fun.

Jack   I did. This is what it's all about.

Linda *almost exits, until:*

Jack   One of the guys told me Edward's working at the FRA.

Linda   Really?

Jack   Yeah, been there a while.

Linda   *Good* – I can finally go back to Starbucks.

Jack   I never imagined he'd go over to the government.

Linda   Maybe he wanted a career change.

Jack   Everyone does now – even people who kept their jobs. The rate of attrition in the City, no one sticks it any more. They all end up in the home counties, everyone I started with . . .

Linda   They burn out.

Jack   They don't have it to begin with. They're just civilians.

Linda   Not everyone's been as lucky as you.

Jack   'Luck'?

Pause.

Linda   Sorry, I didn't mean that. We earned our money. I'm very proud of that, I don't care what the other mothers think.

Jack   I mean the City . . . takes a certain kind of person, a competitive person – and the system works because a small fraction of the population wants to compete, and they succeed. They're the world's engines. They're the ones who make things work. They provide the quality. And . . . I'm just not sure Edward is a quality person.

Linda   That sounds unkind.

Jack   Look at what he's done.

Linda   Be nice. Get some water and go to bed.

Jack   Nine deals in a month. Only 'as good as your last deal'? Read it: *nine.*

Linda   Some men get violent when they're drunk, mine gets cocky.

Jack   No I'm still very wary, lovely, trust me.

Linda   Of what?

Jack   There's one loose end at work I really need to take care of.

Pause.

Jack   Get me dinner with Edward.

Scene Twelve

School rugby pitch.

Fen *and* **Linda** *stand on a touchline, watching Harry play in a school rugby match.* **Linda** *has Violet in a pram.* **Fen** *has a Thermos of coffee for them both.*

While **Linda** *cheers Harry's team on,* **Fen** *has turned away.*

Linda   Go on, ruck over! Come on Fen he's doing really well – GO ON, HARRY!

Fen *turns to look, then turns away again.*

Fen   He's going to get hurt.

Linda   No he's not, he's bigger than all the other boys – Oh! THAT'S IT, HARRY! . . . Nice run.

Fen *looks.*

Fen   Was it?

Linda   Very nice.

Fen   Where is he now?

Linda   At the bottom of that pile.

Fen   Oh God, thanks for coming to this with me.

Linda   I love rugby. All my brothers played.

Fen   I don't understand the rules.

Linda   That's all right, neither do they. That's part of what makes it fun. There goes Harry . . .

They watch. Both of their faces wince with pain – Harry obviously just got smashed.

Linda   Ouch.

Fen   Oh my God.

Linda   He's up, he's running.

Fen *turns her back to the match again.*

Linda   Why did you get him playing?

Fen   The headmistress suggested it. Said it was a 'positive outlet'.

Linda   That's a good idea. And Edward looks good over there in his . . . little rugby shorts.

Fen *turns around and looks for* **Edward**. *They both giggle at him like schoolgirls.*

Fen   He does have nice legs, doesn't he?

Linda   He *is* hot. I don't care where he's from.

Fen   I think it's working, the only problem is . . . the game itself.

Linda   Well then don't watch.

Fen   I feel compelled.

Linda   You shouldn't.

Fen   He's my son. GO HARRY!

A text message tone goes off. **Linda** *checks her mobile.*

Linda   . . . Bloody travel agent.

Fen   Where you going?

Linda   Back to Martha's Vineyard.

Fen   Exciting.

Linda   I get so tired of the South of France in August. You go there, and who do you see? Everyone from London. The people on Martha's Vineyard are much more interesting, and Nantucket Sound is such a secret garden –

Fen   Go on HARRY! COME ON! He should have levelled that bastard.

She realises she interrupted **Linda**.

Fen   That sounds great.

Linda   I hope so. We're staying near the African-American neighbourhood which has a wonderful historical significance. I read about it on the web. There are still guest houses for 'people of colour'.

They watch the match. **Fen** *turns to look at* **Linda** *for some time, without* **Linda** *noticing.*

Linda   Come on!

A whistle blows.

Half time; gosh, he's excellent.

Fen   I'm just glad he's found something – HARRY! HARRY! Come here I've got some slices for you! Harry!

Beat.

Linda   He's pretending not to know you.

Fen   Little bastard.

Linda   How sweet. He's probably going to kill someone in the second half.

Fen   I know. I think he might be all right.

Edward *jogs in from the side wearing his coaching kit. It includes a rugby shirt and rugby shorts.*

Edward   Hiya.

Fen   Hello.

Edward   How's Violet?

Linda   Great thanks.

She can't help but look at **Edward***'s legs while tending to Violet. She starts giggling like a little schoolgirl.*

Fen *hands* **Edward** *a bag of orange slices.*

Fen   Give these to Harry.

Edward   Where are mine?

Fen *looks through her handbag while* **Linda** *checks something on her phone.*

Fen   I didn't . . . Can't you share with Harry?

Edward   He needs these. He's knackered.

Fen (*still looking*)   Well I don't . . . I've got a cough sweet . . .

Linda*'s phone rings. She checks it.*

Linda   I'd better get this.

She exits with the pram, her mobile to her ear. **Edward** *watches* **Linda** *as if waiting for her to get far enough away, and then:*

Edward   Give me the cough sweet.

He takes it and puts it in his mouth.

Fen   Doesn't the coach mind you hanging around?

Edward   No, he likes parents to be assistant coaches.

Fen   It's a public school, Edward, we're paying him to say things like that.

Edward   I'm going to go to coaching school and everything.

Fen   Really?

Edward   Get certified.

Fen   That sounds a bit intense.

Edward   It's hard to get into this coaching school though, quite competitive.

Fen   I'm sure they'll take you; you look so cute.

Edward   *Harry* will like it. Isn't he doing much better?

Fen   Absolutely.

Edward   See the benefits of me getting home early every night?

Fen   You're very sweet and I've finally got some good news for you.

Edward   What's that?

Fen   *Linda.* She's bringing Jack over for dinner Tuesday week.

Edward   Wow.

Fen   She sounded keen . . . We'll see if they actually show up.

Edward   Why wouldn't they?

Fen   How many friends have come for a visit so far?

Edward   We've only been out there a little while . . .

Fen   I keep inviting them but . . .

Edward   People are busy, that's all.

Fen   We live too far away.

Edward   It's like six stops on the District Line.

Fen   But they've never been to Acton.

Edward   A mile difference, two miles.

Fen   I think having to cross Chiswick is a mental barrier for them.

Edward   Do you really want to be friends with people who won't cross Chiswick for you?

Pause.

Fen   I'm just saying.

Edward   Things will get better, just give me some time with this new job. My CV will be perfect –

Fen   Remember the plan.

Edward   Darling I want the same thing you do, okay? This is the way to get there.

Fen   You're always so . . .

Edward   What?

Fen   Cheerful lately.

Edward   I enjoy my job. Today I recommended that a hedge-fund manager be thrown out of the City.

Fen   Why?

Edward   He was lying about his performance figures. A pair of scissors, some glue and a photocopy machine, and he took his investors for £700,000.

Fen   How did you catch him?

Edward   All he needed was someone to look over his shoulder but, you know, there's not really many of us.

Fen   You expect one of those firms to hire you in a year?

Edward   Good people in the City hate all that, too. They've got to compete with these frauds. And in the meantime I get to leave at five o'clock every day.

Fen   Yes –

Edward   I better get over there, hear what the coach is saying. (*With bad Yorkshire accent.*) 'You got to be hard, yeah?'

Beat.

Fen   I moved to Acton.

Edward   I know. You're wonderful.

Fen   If Jack offers you a job you're going to take it. That's the deal.

Edward   Yeah, yeah of course it is.

Fen   So don't enjoy it so much.

Edward   I'm not going to feel guilty about enjoying my new job.

Beat.

Why would I?

Beat.

Why wouldn't I enjoy having a go at the people who screwed it all up for everyone else? I can still make someone pay, for those fuckers who burst my dream. I'M IN CONTROL.

He leaves.

Fen   Edward!

There is no reply.

Linda *comes back with her pram.* **Fen** *smiles at her awkwardly.* **Linda** *fumes.*

Fen   What's wrong?

Linda   We're in a group sponsorship for the Tate and one of the wives just rang – I've never spoken to anyone more bossy in my *life* –

Fen   You're sponsoring the Tate?

Linda   Who does she think she is? How did she even get my number?

Fen *(re: their sponsorship, still shocked)*   Really?

Linda   She's insisting we do a Jackson Pollock show.

Fen *(still shocked)*   Wow.

Linda   Isn't it awful?

Pause.

Fen   I thought Pollock was good.

Linda   Even if he is he's done to death – what hope is there if we can't do someone like Meredith Frampton or John Bratby? Someone *else.*

Beat.

Fen   I don't know.

Linda   And what she said when I told her I wanted Frampton she waited then she said, real slow like she actually knows what she's talking about she said: 'We live in a world of brand' . . . That bitch I'm talking about fucking art. How are we supposed to get out of *this*? Do you mind telling me? How are we supposed to get out of *this trap*?

Beat.

I feel like I could bloody explode. We're talking about a lot of money, a lot of . . . I could just explode.

Scene Thirteen

Edward *and* **Fen***'s dining room in Acton.*

There is a large table where **Edward***,* **Fen***,* **Jack** *and* **Linda** *sit. They've finished eating and are now passing cheese and crackers round.*

Edward *has his head tilted back, and holds a bloody tissue to his nose.*

Edward   The other kids call him 'Tumour'. He's very fat and kind of smells. I pulled him out of a drill and said, 'You're never going to make it as a prop if you don't tackle properly, come practise with me.' So we started practising tackles and then . . . he flattened me.

Linda   Is it getting better?

Edward *brings his head back to normal, but then has quickly to tilt it again.*

Linda   Oh dear.

Fen   I'll get some more tissues.

She leaves, exasperated.

Jack   I never thought rugby was your sport. Always thought you were more of a football man.

Edward   I am, but don't tell Harry that.

Linda   How's he doing?

Edward   The coach thinks he's captain material.

Jack   Amazing.

Edward   He shows real promise. He's brilliant all-round actually, doing better at school –

Linda   We always knew he was a sweet boy.

Edward *brings his head down and takes the tissue away. His nose is okay.*

Edward   He is I think. Deep down.

Fen *enters.*

Fen   Take these just in case. Have some cheese. Be normal.

She sits down nervously and turns to the others.

I hear you've been using your passport a lot this year.

Jack   Tell me about it – where am I?

Linda   He brings the kids home some incredible presents.

Fen   Really?

Jack   I bought a stuffed Komodo dragon for my office.

Fen   Is that legal?

Jack   It is if the dragon has died naturally, although I imagine these Japanese blokes pushing Komodo dragons off a cliff then going 'Whoops'. (*Referring to his mobile.*) Here.

Jack *shows* **Edward** *a photo on his mobile. As soon as* **Edward** *looks at it, he has to tilt his head back. He hands it back to* **Jack** *without looking at him.*

Jack   I'll have to get you one.

Fen   That would be fab.

Edward   They must be horrified, a dragon falling into foreign hands.

Fen   They like English people. Europeans.

Jack   No the Japanese are colour blind: everyone's equally inferior in their eyes.

Linda   We'll have to go see about that. Once we get done with the Americans.

Fen (*to* **Edward**)   They're going to Martha's Vineyard.

Jack   I want to go back to Corsica. Went there on my gap year. I can't go there on business, it's still a bunch of shepherds.

Fen   Oh, Italy . . .

Jack   Corsica is French.

Fen   I know.

Edward   I thought it was all mobsters.

Jack   Yes, shepherds and mobsters. French mobsters.

Fen   Did you get to meet them?

Jack   It can be hard to tell who is a mobster and who isn't. A real mobster's never going to tell you, I mean, look at the royal family.

Fen   Sounds exciting any/way.

Jack   Look at the government, Britain's biggest mob, right Edward? You guys always get your way.

He passes the cheese to **Edward**.

Jack   So how is it over there?

Edward   I like it. And I like the hours.

Jack   You're back in Canary Wharf.

Edward   Yeah, although when I was there before someone brought me coffee four times a day. Now I bring in my own teabags and mark my milk.

Beat.

But I like it.

Jack   Exciting times?

Edward   We'll see.

Jack   So how are you guys gonna solve all the problems then?

Edward   Some more sunlight? It's still the best disinfectant. Let people see the risks they're taking – we used to joke that if the buyer understands what you're doing you're screwed, that you needed something nice and opaque to swing a deal.

Jack   Now, that's a bit reductive.

Edward   Is it? There's teams of people at the bank making this stuff – lawyers and accountants and lawyers from other jurisdictions. It used to be mortgages and now they're doing the same thing with ETFs and gold, credit default swaps . . . But it isn't very long ago, thirty years, banks didn't do this kind of thing at all.

Fen   Eddie, your nose.

Edward *tilts his head back and puts a tissue to it.*

Jack   You're talking the seventies. The stone age.

Edward (*ignoring him*)   I used to have faith things would be okay, real faith, but now . . .

Jack   So you're looking to restrict financial innovation?

Edward   How can I restrict it if I can't understand it? It's just that little bit beyond us. That's where all the genius is.

Jack   Financial innovation is simply the entrepreneurial spirit. It's what makes everything move. The same thing that's given us all of *this*.

He motions around himself. **Edward** *lowers his head. Pause.*

Linda (*to* **Fen**)   Do you really like Acton? Haven't been out this way in ages, not since I met Jack. I had my first flat near Chiswick. And my first real boyfriend was from . . . someplace around there. But I never came back out –

Fen *stands up and begins collecting the dishes.*

Fen   Let me get these out of the way.

Linda *rises and helps.*

Linda   I'll give you a hand.

Edward   How's your art stuff going, is it really happening at the Tate?

Linda *freezes. Awkward silence.*

Linda   We're close to closing the consortium sponsorship.

Fen   Frampton?

Linda   No, Monet. A giant Monet exhibit.

Fen   But I thought you didn't like Monet.

Edward   I thought you fucking hated Monet.

Linda   We all met and I tried I tried but it is a lot of money and there *is* responsibility to . . . succeed with it. Bratby or Frampton who knows what would have . . . At the end of the day it's a real risk, a lot of money –

Jack   A *lot* of money . . .

Linda   To try something else when we . . . So that was it and I've told you so can we not talk art please? Let's just fucking ignore it please.

Beat. **Linda** *marches into the kitchen with some dishes.* **Fen** *quietly follows.*

Long silence. **Jack** *is unfazed.*

Jack   I like your enthusiasm.

Edward   Thanks.

Jack   Sounds like it's given you a different angle on things.

Edward   Yeah, and gives me time to be beaten up by twelve-year-olds.

Jack   That is extraordinary.

Edward   Not really, Tumour's centre of gravity is lower than mine. And much bigger.

Jack   But Harry's enjoying it.

Edward   Yes.

Jack   And Kathy?

Edward   She's good. They're still there, anyway.

Jack   What do you mean? Is everything okay?

Edward   Yeah we're fine. We've joined the school's new 'recession payment plan for distressed parents'.

Jack   That's great.

Edward   Yeah. It's a thrill a minute.

Pause. **Jack** *takes a good look at* **Edward***.*

Jack   I'm so sorry for being so busy, falling out of touch . . . Linda's been telling me for months that you're looking for a job, been in the back of my mind. I thought of it right after Lehman. Now that you've got one . . . are you sure you don't want to come back to the private sector? Things can only get better.

Edward   You're right on that one.

Jack   It's certainly a good time to sow the seeds for the next boom, the race is on . . . This is when rich people become *really* rich; I can see everyone with cash buying up assets, struggling companies . . .

Edward   Must be fun, you getting in on it?

Jack   I'm trying to make a go, using my contacts, and some business partners to count on. Some quality people.

Edward   Great, like who?

They look at each other.

Jack   Like John Woolrich.

Beat.

Edward   Right.

Jack   He's a management director for Seven Woods Capital.

Edward   I heard you twice the first time.

Jack   He's a good businessman –

Edward (*laughs*)   We don't really think so at the FRA.

Jack   It's a dubious charge, honestly.

Edward   The guy was lying about performance figures with scissors and glue.

Jack   That's an exagger/ation.

Edward   And nothing compared to what we're finding now – there were other dubious goings-on at Seven Woods.

Jack   He just hit a bit of a rough patch, you don't need to –

Edward   The paper trail will convict him: it's a clear-cut case. His brother-in-law tipped him off about that takeover, Woolrich bought in big and made a fortune.

Jack   He's a very smart guy. He could have come to that conclusion all on his own. And he's a friend of mine, okay?

Pause.

Edward   Is this why you're finally coming over to my house?

Jack   No of course not, I only wanted to say that fair is fair: you know the FRA has never successfully prosecuted an insider dealing case.

Edward   My guess is that Mr Woolrich will be the first.

Jack   Will you argue his side at the FRA? You're getting on well there.

Edward *tilts his head back and applies the tissue.*

Edward   I'm just a foot soldier / really

Jack   That's not what people are saying.

Edward *lowers his head, slowly.*

Edward   What do you, have spies there?

Jack   He doesn't deserve this. He's a good man.

Edward   It will be minimum security, he'll probably get to leave on weekends.

Beat.

Jack   You know I never forgot about you. It wasn't like that.

Edward   Good to hear.

He tilts his head back.

But it's open-and-shut, nothing I can do. The FRA is really excited about this – high-profile, glamorous, breaking new ground in prosecution. And maybe there were other beneficiaries, too, outside of his family. Who knows?

He lowers his head, morbidly. He's put two and two together.

But surely not you.

Jack   It's a delicate situation.

Edward   'Delicate'?

Jack   You're telling me you never took a tip? You know what it's like out there, it's vicious right now. I needed –

Edward   You seem to be doing well for yourself. Is all your success coming from inside information –

Jack   No, *no* not at all. I just saw him at a corporate jolly, at a couple of things, we had a chat . . . I saw a chance to boost my quarter and I took it. I just did it one day. Because that's business – and . . . you've got to let Woolrich off scot-free. Because you're right, if you go through with it . . . my name will come up. I'm at the end of the paper trail, along with God-knows-who else. It's like getting busted in a whorehouse, the same one everyone else uses . . .

Edward   Jack, I don't know what to say, but . . .

Jack   But what? We go back to Lehman together –

Edward   Oh God – that's your pitch?

Jack   To before that to before . . . I was just some twenty-one-year-old medic when I met you –

Edward   What are you saying? 'We knew each other in the nineties, let me break the law'?

Jack   No mate it's because when we met . . . I mean you go and you *meet someone* and you think, 'Oh my God, okay, here we are, there's another mind in the room, it's not just me, this is a real person', because most of us are, by default, entirely . . . Other people do not impinge enough on our experience of life, they just drift past and they say the expected things, and so when someone impinges, when someone breaks through and strikes you with something you hadn't thought before it is a joy, Edward.

Beat.

And that's why I left medicine, because I met you. That's why I applied to Lehman and every other bank in the City, you fucking muppet, *you*.

Edward   Maybe it was an obvious choice, you'd just been missing your chances.

Jack   It was a great favour. And we live in a world where people do each other favours.

Pause.

Jack   I'm offering you a job Edward. Save Woolrich, and I'll bring you on board when the dust clears.

Edward   Right.

Jack   Competitive salary and bonus. At *First Brook*.

Edward   First Brook.

Jack   And for what?

Edward   I don't have that kind of sway.

Jack   I've done my homework on this one. And I know in a room of thirty people, Edward is going to have some sway.

Edward   Maybe I don't want your job.

Jack   You / don't −

Edward   *Yeah*, I'm in a good place right now. I've got time to be with my family, Harry's getting better.

Jack   You can have those things too. And the job.

Edward *lowers his head.*

Edward   I'm not sure I want to go back. I actually like my job, I can see −

Jack   Christ, you're not going to get on a soapbox are you? What if Harry's entire class cheated on an exam, and only he got caught − do you think he's the one that should be punished?

Edward   What are you talking about?

Jack   I'm talking about the real world.

Edward   Yeah Lehman evaporated in an instant, ten years of stock options *gone*.

Jack   What I'm saying is to think about your family, their future.

Edward   I am: just by having some more time, my son is getting better.

Jack   His school can sort him out. Send him anywhere you want.

Edward   But I think it's my fault he was bad. All those compromises.

Jack   You need to do this. For him. It will come back to help all of you.

Edward   I don't want it.

Jack   This is *everything* you want. For you, your kids, Fen . . . They love you. And they just want things to be normal again. I'm offering you a step *up*.

Edward   Yes.

Jack   We're on then.

No response.

We're on. All charges against him dropped.

Beat.

Edward   I don't know.

Pause. **Linda** *enters from kitchen.*

Linda   Can you call us a cab?

Edward   It's fifteen minutes on the tube.

Linda   I don't want to take the tube.

She throws herself on a chair.

Jack   I know I can count on you.

Linda   A *taxi*. I want a taxi. I want to go home now.

Jack   I can count on the Edward I *remember*.

Edward (*to* **Jack**)   We'll see.

Act Two

Scene Fourteen

Sir Roger*'s office, First Brook Capital.*

Sir Roger   You can't be charged!

Jack   I'm *not* going to be charged.

Pause.

Jack   I *might* be charged. I don't know.

Sir Roger   Our investors are fucking nervous like the rest of
the world and now I'm going to have the FRA in here going
through all our books, interviewing my people, smearing our
name in the press –

Jack   It will blow over.

Sir Roger   Reputation is everything in this business.

Jack   Is it?

Sir Roger *stands up in disgust at this remark and pours himself a
whisky.*

Jack   Are you going to stand by me?

Sir Roger *pours another whisky and hands it to* **Jack**.

Sir Roger   You made a mistake.

Jack   I'm sorry.

Sir Roger   Well then . . . it's a good thing you're indispensable.

He chinks glasses with **Jack**.

And innocent, right?

They drink.

Jack   Yes.

Sir Roger   Of course, if they convict you your career's history and we never met.

Emma *buzzes.*

Emma (*voice*)   Your one o'clock is here.

Sir Roger   And work doesn't stop just because you've picked up a stench.

Jack *stands.*

Sir Roger   Stick around, this person is just your type.

Emma *returns, followed by* **Kim**.

Sir Roger   Kimberly Lopez?

Kim   Kim.

Sir Roger   Roger Glynn.

They shake hands. **Kim** *does not shake hands with* **Jack**.

Sir Roger   Goldman Sachs. Green Forest…

Kim   Yes.

Sir Roger   So what can I do for you?

Kim   I was recently gathering investment to bid on a couple companies . . .

Sir Roger   I read the documents you sent. This is exactly the kind of thing we've been doing, very nice. So what do you need, some help?

Kim   No, I was all ready to do these deals on my own, I've already raised the funding . . .

Sir Roger   And?

Kim   I realised I was wasting my time.

Sir Roger   Why? They looked shrewd. Perfect.

Kim   They'll provide a tidy profit, but that's when I realised: all these collapsing firms are small fry when you consider

Britain's banks. The world's largest bankrupt institutions, and now's the time to make a move on them.

Pause.

Sir Roger   You're having a laugh.

Kim   Think about it: in America there's a stimulus plan building roads and schools, but here it's just the banks getting money in that massive bailout.

Sir Roger   Okay.

Kim   But the UK bailout hasn't worked, share prices are collapsing, investors are paranoid because Northern Rock and Bear Stearns are long gone and they saw Lehman sink. So if you're Lloyds or RNBS, do you really believe the government is going to save you with a second bailout? It's still a totally chaotic situation, so . . .

Sir Roger   Yes?

Kim   A lot of people own bonds from those two busted banks.

Sir Roger   Too bad for them. They'll probably never make their money back.

Kim   I want to sell them credit default swaps.

Sir Roger *considers.*

Jack   That's crazy. Sell swaps on those bonds? Too risky – the media would have a field day.

Kim   You don't know that.

Jack   We'll end up in the papers for gambling on a defunct RNBS, and if we *succeed* then we'd be making money off a collapsed bank. The press would kill us for it. Roger, you can't touch this, no way.

Sir Roger   I don't know . . . Emma?

Emma   Yes?

Sir Roger   What do you think?

Emma   Of what?

Jack   You're going to ask your PA?

Sir Roger (*to* **Jack**)   Shut up. You want to know what the public thinks, she *is* the public.

Emma   I never really . . .

Sir Roger *sits* **Emma** *down and stands to one side of her, with* **Jack** *on the other. She looks a bit like a judge between two lawyers.*

Sir Roger   Just keep an open mind, all right? Rich people and companies buy bonds from RNBS that pay them interest every year –

Emma   Yeah, I get that part.

Sir Roger   But there's a problem over the ten years you own the bond. The bank may not survive. If it goes under you'll lose everything you paid for your bond, you're very worried –

Kim   And then I come along: you pay me a fee every year, and then if the bank defaults I will pay out the full value of your bond.

Emma   You sell me an insurance policy.

Kim   Exactly.

Kim *picks up* **Sir Roger**'*s* (*now empty*) *whisky glass.*

Kim   Let's say this glass is our agreement. It makes you feel safe. So you're not concerned at all if RNBS goes under because now you know you'll get the money from me anyway.

Emma   That sounds great.

Kim   But when that insurance agreement is a credit default swap, I don't have to hold on to our agreement, it's tradable. So I sell our agreement to someone else for a one-off fee.

Kim *hands the glass to* **Sir Roger**.

Kim   Now your insurance payments go to *him*, and *he's* the one who will pay out to you if RNBS defaults on your bond.

Emma   Why did you do that? Why didn't you keep it like a nice simple insurance agreement?

Kim   That glass is more of a bet – I bet you that RNBS will survive. If I lose the bet I pay out the full value of your bond. If I win the bet I collect your insurance premiums and don't pay out a cent. I place a lot of bets on what will happen – I create more glasses like this one. I can sell these bets to other people who are keen to take them on, get in on the action. Over time, one bet can pass through dozens of hands. If the government *does* decide to underwrite RNBS, the person holding this glass down the daisy chain is a lucky winner: there is now *zero* risk of default, and they still get to collect your insurance premiums until this contract (*motioning to the glass*) ends.

Emma   Who will that be?

Kim (*shrugs*)   Who knows who'll be holding this glass by then.

Jack   But if RNBS *does* go under, whoever's holding this glass down the daisy chain will have to pay up. Who's going to take that risk? If we make these swaps – (*grabbing the glass*) no one is going to want to buy them from us – we'll be left holding this crap. And then if RNBS defaults we go bankrupt overnight.

Kim *grabs the glass.*

Kim   But what if we make these swaps and then sell them on to RNBS? Sell them to the 'risky bank' itself?

Emma   I don't . . . How is RNBS going to pay out my insurance if they go under?

Kim   If they go under, they won't have to pay out. They won't be *able* to pay out.

She holds up the glass.

They look to **Sir Roger** *for a reaction, but he doesn't give one.*

Kim   RNBS bondholders are so terrified right now, they'll jump at the chance to insure their stuff. You worked at RNBS, you still know everyone there, and the swaps we make will be easy to sell on to RNBS because if they go broke, they won't have to pay out on any of them.

Emma   Is that legal?

Kim   It isn't *illegal* yet.

Sir Roger *takes the glass back from* **Kim** *and studies it.*

Emma (*to* **Sir Roger**)   Roger, I've decided. You shouldn't do this.

Sir Roger   Thank you Emma . . . but I'm feeling some serious deal heat.

Jack   Roger! You can't honestly think of −

Sir Roger   I'm not going to just stand on the touchlines.

Jack   But −

Sir Roger   But what? Use your fucking brain, it's not there *just* to make your head heavy. Kim − lunch?

He opens the door, still carrying the glass.

He and **Kim** *leave together.*

Emma *now looks very commanding in* **Sir Roger**'*s chair.*

Emma   Impressive . . . and it's my verdict that you're probably second best now.

Jack *sits down, stunned.*

Jack   Rubbish.

Emma   *Shame.*

Jack   You've been jealous of my success since I got here.

Emma   You're not a success, you've just been running through raindrops. Now you're about to get wet.

Jack *looks at* **Emma**. *She stands up authoritatively and exits, snapping the door behind her.*

Scene Fifteen

The FRA.

Edward *is working away at his desk.* **Chris** *enters carrying an empty glass and looking a bit harried.*

Chris   Jesus . . . say hello to a war hero coming from the Eastern Front.

Edward   You all right?

Chris   Yeah – we got Woolrich in there.

Edward *leaps from his desk.*

Edward   You've got Woolrich in there?! *Really?* Why wasn't I told?

Chris *(realising his mistake, blocking* **Edward**'s *path)*   Oh – shit, mate. You're to stay away, all right?

Edward   What the fuck is this? Let me *at him* –

Chris   You're staying away from all this.

Edward   No I'm not –

Chris   Yeah you are.

Edward   Fuck off.

Chris   You've got a conflict of interests, give it a rest.

Edward   What 'conflict'?

Chris   That guy we want to charge is a friend of yours.

Edward   Old colleague.

Chris   So you're keeping a safe distance from Woolrich, okay?

Edward   Fuck that. The investigation is mine –

Chris   That was before we knew.

Edward   Who cares?

Chris   Wouldn't be professional mate.

Edward   Really?

Chris Yeah.

Edward I'll take my chances. We've *got* to turn Woolrich – that's the key, we need him as a fucking *witness* for everything else –

Chris We're working on it.

Edward I'm out . . . of my own case? How do *you* decide what I do and what I don't –

Chris You got to calm down. It's not your decision to make. Take it or leave it.

Pause. **Edward** *collects himself.*

Chris Just *cheer up* – we're in there, we're crawling right up his arse. This guy's seat is getting very uncomfortable. He's sweating.

Edward He is?

Chris He's got the yellow legal pad out, he's writing things down on it. Fuck me if I know what.

Edward Probably dirty jokes for his lawyer to see.

Chris That's the thing: he came alone.

Edward *Alone?*

Chris Solo.

Edward People like him don't go anywhere alone.

Chris He came here without a lawyer.

Edward He just *showed up* –

Chris And he sits down with his attitude, like he's pissed off there's no sweet dish on the table. So I say 'Would you like some water' and he says . . . 'Yes,' just like that. He picks up his glass and holds it out to me. I don't say anything. He keeps holding the empty glass out. So I say 'I'm not a waiter, cheers.'

Edward You said that?

Chris No. I don't say anything. He keeps –

Edward Yeah.

Chris   But he's not even blinking. I'm not going to – he says, finally he says, 'Please'. Like I'm putting him out by making him speak. He starts fingering his phone. He's trying to seem too busy for us. He wants out, he's like, 'I just want to emphasise how I came here today voluntarily.'

Edward   'Voluntary'? It's *statutory*.

Chris   And I'm like, 'You came into this thing with your eyes wide open. Don't start crying blind man now.'

Edward   You said that?

Chris   No. I said I'd get him some water.

Edward   Where's Henry? I'd like a fucking word.

Chris   I've told you to leave it. I've told you officially –

Edward   This is *my case.*

Chris   You're new and you're doing a great job. Don't try to be a superhero. That's not our culture here.

Edward   Don't be ridiculous.

Chris   You're skilled, but I've been here eight years.

Edward   You're crazy. I'll go to Henry.

Chris   He's busy –

Edward   – with cases I'm building!

Chris   Why insist on working a case where you have a clear conflict of interests?

Edward   Because there *is* no conflict.

Chris   Jack Tilly is a friend of yours.

Edward   An old colleague. And I don't fucking care –

Chris   I do –

Edward   Because we're building something here. Because I'm going to make someone pay for what happened. So it's a mate? *Even better.*

Scene Sixteen

A posh, trendy restaurant.

Kim *and* **Henry** *chink glasses of red wine and drink.*

Henry   Is Ben Colchurch still in Goldman's M&A –

Kim   Yes oh my God he was my boss actually. Do you know him?

Henry   He was my trainee. He stood outside my door for a year.

Kim   At Goldman?

Henry   *No*, we started at the same merchant bank. Good old Benny.

Kim   Yes.

Henry   Wonderful energy.

Kim   You could say so.

Henry   He stood outside my door very . . . attentively. For a little toad.

Kim *laughs, a little too much.* **Henry** *enjoys it.*

Henry   Does he still write poetry?

Kim *laughs again.*

Kim   Yes. It's mandatory reading.

Henry   I'm sorry to hear that . . . You know, you miss torturing someone like that little wart.

He takes a sip of wine.

Kim   Any warts at the FRA?

Henry   Of course not! It's all very . . . pleasant. Very pleasant. As is the wine.

Kim *swishes and smells hers.*

Kim   It's very fruit-forward, right on the tip of your tongue. Almost . . . plum.

Henry *sips again.*

Kim   Was this a really wet year? Was there a lot of rain that year?

Henry   I don't know.

Kim *sips, then sighs contentedly.*

Kim   (*looking around*) I love it in this place. There was someone really famous in here the other day. I don't know his name.

Henry   Right.

Kim   When I was working for myself I had all my meetings here.

Beat.

Not that this is a meeting. We were just hoping to have a conversation. If Mr Tilly is going to be formally charged?

Henry   Yes . . .

Beat.

He is. I think.

Pause.

You didn't stay at Goldman −

Kim   No. I wanted to broaden my horizons. I went to Green Forest.

Henry   Nice people there.

Kim   We were quite a tightly knit team. *You* really broadened your horizons, what took you to the FRA?

Henry (*shrugs*)   When certain people in your life ring you, you pick up the phone don't you? And they said to me 'We need your help'. I'll never forget it I always believed in public service, that public life is a noble pursuit, can still be, even knowing everything we *do* about politicians. It can still be a good thing and . . . you know . . . even my wife went for the idea – *wha-hey*.

Kim   That's great.

Henry   Mmm . . .

She pours him more wine.

Kim   We're just a little concerned about any undeserved scrutiny or smear Jack Tilly could bring upon First Brook.

Henry   Such as?

Kim   The FRA coming in, checking everything, getting interviews, disrupting our reputation – we're at quite a sensitive moment with the markets, all that chaos and bad press could really impair the fund's –

Henry   I would say, given the current situation –

Kim   Which I don't know anything about. I've been with First Brook for a while now and I've never even met Jack Tilly.

Henry   No?

Kim   I'm not even sure Sir Roger really knows who he is. I mean he probably knows Jack's *face* but ultimately Jack Tilly was just very . . . rogue.

Henry   But it's not just Jack Tilly.

Kim   Excuse me?

Henry   I said it's not just this mess with Tilly. We've had our eye on First Brook for some time.

Kim   . . . What about it?

Henry   I'm saying that it is possible to sail close to the wind once. You can sail close to the wind twice, maybe even three times . . . But when it gets to four or five times, it becomes a regular pattern of behaviour, you do have to ask questions about the navigational skills of those on the bridge.

Beat.

Kim   I see. But I'm sure it's just a misunderstanding –

Henry   I'm sure it's just a few misunderstandings, but when Tilly is charged there is at least a chance he'll be convicted, so someone like Sir Roger needs to think about whether he is capable of leading substantive change substantively, and also whether the external world would perceive that, because I think perception is part of the reality in these circumstances. And right now the perception is not good.

Beat.

I can tell you it is not good with the external world.

Kim   That's very helpful. Thank you. But I think it's like the classic children's tale, there is a danger to crying 'wolf' when no moral risk exists. We become so inured to the parade of over-hyped misdeeds that we fail to react appropriately when the real wolf appears.

Pause.

I wouldn't say we're clean clean but I'd say we're clean in principle.

Henry   Hmm . . . I appreciate that. Ta.

He takes a sip of wine to end the topic of conversation. **Kim** *awkwardly follows.*

Kim   What happens if Cameron gets in next month?

Henry   What happens for me? Or what happens to people like you?

No response as he sees through her question.

Haven't you been listening? 'The Tory Party is the party to bring law and order to financial markets.'

No response. He drinks.

Dark stone fruits, that's what I'm getting.

Scene Seventeen

The FRA.

A table with many chairs, and many documents spread out upon it.

Henry, **Chris**, **Jack** *and* **Jack's Lawyer** *sit at it.*

Jack   It's really very simple. And I was coming off a rough year like everyone else.

Chris   I'm glad you came out of it. I'm glad the stock you bought in that company really paid off after the merger.

Jack's Lawyer   My client is not –

Chris   Just tell me why you bought so much stock in that company.

Pause.

Okay?

Jack *looks at his* **Lawyer** *warily.*

Jack   Seemed like a good idea.

Henry   Why?

Jack   The market.

Henry   What did the market tell you, exactly? What did you see?

Jack   The market is the market.

Henry   All we're saying, as *politely* as possible, is that all pieces fit together. Chris?

Chris *distributes identical files.*

Chris   Meetings in restaurants, telephone calls, trading patterns with an odd surge.

Jack's Lawyer   Circumstantial.

Henry   All that's needed –

Jack's Lawyer   To bring charges? Fine but you won't win. My client will be able to explain all of this in a court of law −

Henry   He'd better do a good job −

Jack's Lawyer   *More* than capably − he was responding to the market, while all you can offer is porous, circumstantial evidence.

Henry   Be that as it may, Part 5, Schedule 1 of / the Criminal −

Edward *enters.*

Henry   Edward.

Jack's Lawyer   To charge him? Fine, but a criminal conviction for insider trading has never been obtained by the FRA, and for good legal reason: you need a co-operating witness, and you haven't got one. So can we please move through these hypotheticals as quickly as possible? They don't change the *fact* that my client will be a hero once he stands up to unfair allegations and heavy-handed −

Henry   We'll take our chances.

Edward (*to* **Henry**)   I've been meaning to give you this.

Henry   What is it?

Jack   Hello Edward.

Edward   We got Woolrich on-side.

Pause.

Jack's Lawyer   John Woolrich is giving evidence against my client?

Edward   Yeah. He's cut himself a bit of a deal. Here's his deposition.

Edward *hands these out.* **Henry** *and* **Chris** *are as surprised as the others.* **Jack's Lawyer** *looks at the deposition fearfully, while* **Jack** *doesn't bother: he just stares at* **Edward***.*

Jack's Lawyer (*reading*)   There's a conflict of interest here, of course.

Jack (*still staring at* **Edward**)   Absolutely.

Jack's Lawyer (*reading*)   Woolrich is just trying to save his own skin.

Henry   Hmm . . . Thank you Edward.

Chris (*reading*)   'Jenny Finch, Simon Foster, Naresh Padel . . . ' (*To* **Jack**.) And you.

Henry   Is there anything you'd like to add?

Jack's Lawyer   No . . . no . . . Not until I've had a closer look.

He stands. **Jack** *follows.*

Jack's Lawyer   We'll be in touch . . . after (*i.e. 'after I've had a closer look'.*)

They leave. **Henry** *is about to follow but comes back to the table.*

Henry   You CHEEKY BUGGER.

Chris   What the fuck was that?

Edward   I got skills, all right? I nailed him.

Chris   How?

Edward   I ran into him. I convinced him to have a coffee with me. That it would be in his self-interest.

Henry   And?

Edward   And then I brought him in.

Henry *is pressed for time, he heads for the door.*

Henry   My office in twenty minutes.

He leaves.

Chris   Where would you 'run into' Woolrich?

Edward   Does it really matter? I got a result.

Silence. He gives up and heads for door.

Chris   Nice work big man.

He leaves.

Edward *clears up his stuff from the table.*

Jack *comes back in. He shuts the door behind him.*

Edward *hears the door close and looks up. He sees* **Jack***.*

Jack   Why?

Edward (*shrugs*)   They caught Woolrich red-handed and he's paranoid we'll make an example out of him. He's selling everyone out.

Jack   And me?

Edward   You're a casualty. I'm sorry. There's nothing I could do.

Jack   'Nothing you could do'?

Edward   I'm not the one who got into bed with John Woolrich. Don't bitch to me now that you're pregnant.

Jack   I offered you a fucking deal – a *job*, a great job and this is how you –

Edward   This is the FRA, it needed this – People can't invest in our stock market unless they think it has integrity, right? It's that basic –

Jack   Since when did you become such a cunting radical?!

Edward   Don't make this personal.

Jack   Ruining my career, making me a –

Edward   *You* ruined it. There's nothing I could do.

Jack   Can't you even lie any more?

Edward   The game's changing.

Jack   *I'm* the fucking change? I don't want to be –

Edward   We'll see.

Pause.

Jack   Get me out of this. I can't – Linda and the kids.

Edward   They'll still love you. Take it on the chin –

Jack   'Love me'? I'm not talking about love. I don't want them to *suffer* – I don't want them to feel ashamed – broke and ashamed. Doesn't that – can't you understand that a little bit? Does that get through at all?

Edward   Of course it does.

Jack   I'm begging you – Help me, cut me a deal – You cut Woolrich a deal *I* want a fucking deal. I'm begging you.

Edward   Like what?

Jack   Sir Roger. I'll tell you something he's doing right now. Something new something's fucked and you can take him down – he's ripping off bondholders. Nail him and get me off.

Edward   You want to give evidence on First Brook?

Jack   Do you see them riding to my rescue here? They fucking abandoned me –

Edward   And you'll go all the way with it?

Jack   They've wanted to cut my balls off from the beginning –

Edward   If you do, I'll get you off –

Jack   You promise?

Edward   I *can* do that. And I'll go all the way for you. I promise.

Scene Eighteen

School rugby pitch.

Fen *faces the audience, cheering on her son's rugby team.*

Fen   HARRY! Come on Harry – ruck over! HARRY! GET THERE!

Edward *arrives. He is wearing his coaching kit.*

Edward   What are you doing over here?

Fen   What do you mean?

Edward   Everyone else is on the other touchline.

Fen   Yes.

Edward   So?

Fen   That's kind of the point.

Edward   Why?

Fen   Carolyn's over there . . . and Lindsay . . . and that awful estate agent who comes to every match.

Edward   Go on, say hi to Carolyn

Fen   I don't want to. I came here to get away from them.

Edward   Why?

Fen   Because I don't like them. I never did. I'm only realising it now.

Edward   Their children are Harry's *friends* – he goes to their birthday parties.

Fen   Then why don't we move?

Edward   What?

Fen   Out of London.

Edward   We live in Acton.

Fen   I'm mean someplace further out, away from all this.

Edward   Umm . . . no. Why do you ask?

Fen   Oh! Don't worry, I'm happy in Acton. There's a lot of great people there, actually, and they do things like . . .

Edward Have coffee?

Fen Well yes they have coffee but they talk about things, things I don't know anything about: Bon Jovi, the prison – one of them has a husband who's a parole officer.

Edward Wow.

Fen The stories she tells about it.

Edward Yeah, I can imagine.

Fen That's the thing, you think you know and then… you don't –

Edward HARRY! Come on! Lower, like I showed you! PUSH! (*To* **Fen**.) Are you scared of going back over there?

Fen Why?

Edward Because Jack's been charged and my fingerprints are all over it. Even that estate agent's been giving me the evil eye. Like *I'm* the one who's sinned –

Fen So stay over here.

Edward Did one of them make a comment to you or something?

Fen I wouldn't care if they did.

Edward Jack will get off – I promised him I'm going to sort it out.

Fen *Edward*. It doesn't matter.

Edward Well if they *knew* maybe they wouldn't –

Fen Eddie I don't care. I don't care what they think. I'm really happy. The kids are doing great, we *see* you. We all have breakfast together every morning.

Edward With no newspapers, no computers.

Fen No phones.

Edward That's nice, isn't it?

Fen   And then we have dinner at six.

Edward   Six sharp. I forgot what a good cook you are.

Fen   I love you.

They hug.

You just missed the headmistress – *she* came over to this side to say hello.

Edward   Did she ask you if we're going to pay on time? I'll kill her –

Fen   No –

Edward   You know her famous 'recession payment plan' isn't all it's cracked up to be, one missed payment with that battleaxe and –

He makes the throat-cutting gesture.

Fen   It wasn't about money this time. The teachers want to give Harry an award, at the end of term.

Edward   For what?

Fen   For his improvement you wally.

Edward   Really?

Fen   GO ON, KEEP GOING!

Edward   Fuck me. Really?

Fen *nods.*

Fen   So maybe we can go away at half-term, for a couple days? He deserves –

Edward   When I'm still trying to pay the bloody school?

Fen   Oh yeah, sorry.

Edward   There's been a lot of money going out even though we're settled and . . .

Fen   So what are we going to do?

Edward   I don't know.

Pause.

Fen   Why don't we just sell that bracelet gave me?

Beat.

Edward   Why the bracelet? It was your anniversary present and . . .

Fen   Could you sell it?

Beat.

Edward   I don't know.

Fen   Could you get what you paid for it?

Edward   I doubt it.

Pause. They watch the match.

Fen   They could just go to school in Acton you know.

Edward   Acton?

Fen   It's a solution –

Edward   Now? When Harry's getting an award and everything?

Fen   But still, is it really worth it?

Edward *makes a disapproving noise.*

Fen   What?

Edward *shakes his head.*

Fen   I don't understand.

Edward   I know you don't.

Fen   What would they really be missing if they weren't with them? (*The people on the other side of the pitch.*)

Edward   The question is 'where would they be?' The answer is easy: *nowhere*. Nowhere at all – I want them pushed. I don't want them just sitting around –

Fen   I know.

Pause. They watch the match.

Edward   And I'm sorry about half-term. It's rubbish I know.

Fen   We'll do something together. It'll be nice.

They kiss.

And I *am* proud of you, really, that you're doing what you're doing.

Edward   Things will get better. For us.

They turn back to the match:

HARRY COME ON! GO HARRY YES RUN!

Fen   GO HARRY COME ON!

They watch.

Edward   Oh come on ref no way – no way ref! HE DIDN'T DO IT!

As **Edward** *starts to exit,* **Linda** *steps onstage blocking his path. If looks could kill.*

Edward (*to* **Linda**)   Hey.

Fen   Linda.

No response.

Edward (*to* **Linda**)   I've made Jack a promise.

Scene Nineteen

The FRA.

Henry, **Edward** *and* **Chris** *at a table covered in documents.*

Behind **Chris** *is a bulletin board, like the kind police use when tracing a gang.*

In the centre of the bulletin board is written the name 'John Woolrich' – surrounded by a complex web of names and transactions. One of the names on the board is 'Jack Tilly'.

Henry *studies the board.*

Henry   One two three four five six seven eight nine ten eleven . . . How many of these people benefited from Woolrich?

Edward   That we could prosecute? I'd say four.

Henry   Out of all this?

Edward   There's more but most is . . .

Chris   Circumstantial.

Henry   Well four is brilliant – we've never done this before. I'm delighted.

Edward   Thanks, but the best part is what's come down through Jack Tilly.

Henry   Of course. I got your email on that. Very interesting.

Edward   And big. Massive. I offered to let Jack off with a formal warning if we can –

Henry (*ignoring* **Edward***)*   *Great.* That's great – but we'll be keeping Jack in with the other three; we'll be prosecuting him fully.

Edward   You saw my – all that came from Jack – about the credit default swaps, RNBS, First Brook – he's giving us full information.

Henry   Yes yes of course I *saw* it we're not *pursuing* it. That's a dead duck and so's Jack. Include him with the others for prosecution.

Edward   *Why?* Look what he did – what he's giving us.

Henry   We won't be pursuing that.

Edward   First Brook Capital is selling these swaps, en masse, to generate huge revenue –

Henry   What's your point?

Edward   My point is that RNBS issued those bonds in the first place and is now providing insurance on them. Can you see why I'm worried? No one knows, and this game's gotten into the hundreds of millions.

No response.

I'm saying there's something spoiled in the state of Denmark.

Henry   'Rotten'. 'There's something rotten in the state of Denmark'.

Edward   If RNBS defaults, it can't pay out the guarantee because it's *already broke*. And the reason it's broke is because of instruments just like this!

Henry   We don't make the rules, remember that. We enforce them. Technically, what Sir Roger is doing is legal.

Edward   But what about the bondholders?

Henry   What *about* the bondholders . . .

Edward   Do they know the guarantees they bought are now meaningless?

Henry   Think about what you're saying: if we bust this up to protect the insurance on those bonds, what we'll *actually* be saying is that those bondholders need some insurance. We would be saying that RNBS, the bank that has now been bailed out by taxpayers, is still at real risk of defaulting. We'll support the market's fears. We'll hurt the bank even more. We – the three of us in this room – could make another, very expensive bailout a necessity. That will cost the taxpayer more money. So we have to leave it alone or we'll make a default much *more* likely, not less. *We'll* scare people. People are scared enough already. And our system requires that people are not scared.

Edward   In the meantime Sir Roger makes a killing.

Henry   We want to keep people calm, assure them – at some level – that the markets are functioning, you don't take down Roger Glynn –

Edward   What about Jack Tilly? John Woolrich?

Henry   High-profile, *small-stakes* cases, so find me some more of those. Bloody perfect.

Edward   This could be good. Let me dig –

Henry   He's too big. Drop it.

Edward   What are you, afraid?

Henry   Practical. He's an offshore guy living in an offshore world. Get over it.

Edward   You're telling us to change things. Since Cameron got in, *he's* telling us to change / things –

Henry   What do you want?

Edward   A pair of bollocks around here – what are you telling me, there's a glass ceiling to this job? I can only go so far with it?

Henry   'Everything in moderation'.

Edward   Don't pull a public school escape hatch please –

Henry   Ah shut up –

Edward   – I just want *us*, this place, to be able to . . . compete, take a decent *look* at what they're doing, hold them legally account/able –

Henry   It *is* legal!

Edward   I want to investigate –

Henry   It *looks* legal. So drop it. Sir Roger's at the top, transnational. Press on him too hard and he's gone. Do you really want First Brook Capital and its £20 billion to disappear to the Caymans?

Edward Do we want him *here* ripping people off? People with jobs, who buy homes and –

Henry Homes that are worth something because there's still money kicking around this country.

Pause.

Why do you think companies move to London in the first place? The food? Funny accents? The Queen? They only come because of the *freedom* – move your money through London and we won't ask you were it comes from. We won't ask what you're doing with it, we just hope some of it will stick here. And a lot of times it works. Everyone knows that Britain and British colonies – Hong Kong, the Caymans, Jersey – are safe, we maintain that aura of respectability – without asking too many questions. So foreigners want to park their money here, enjoy our perfect combination of stability and freedom. You want change fine but don't fuck up the winning combination – stay under your glass ceiling and like it! Have a cup of fucking tea and talk about your favourite cricket team, sponsored by Barclays! We need the finance game. We *want* Sir Roger here. There's nothing else.

Henry leaves.

Edward What are you fucking mute?! Why didn't you tell him?

Chris When I tried to run the case, you told me to fuck off. Now you want me to get involved?

Edward Of course I do! We're on the same side!

Chris We're a team. No superheroes.

Edward Fuck off –

Chris And I'm telling you he's right. You'll go far and change things but you got to pick your battles.

Pause.

Edward I did. I made a promise.

Scene Twenty

Headmistress's office.

Edward *sits across from* **Paula**, *the headmistress of Harry and Kathy's school.*

Paula   We really do sympathise with the emotional connection families build with the school, which is why we created the payment plan, but even a school like ours can only finance so much –

Edward   It's just this one payment, it's just a little late and then it will be fine. I've got the money com/ing.

Paula   We've approached the limit I'm afraid, as an institution, there's just no money, no more money for this kind / of

Edward   You're honouring our son for good behaviour for Christ's sake –

Paula   With the missed payment we've taken quite a close look at you, the bursar and myself and, well . . . you represent a risk, a significant risk, we're not sure we can carry you any longer –

Edward   And I hope I've made myself useful to the school, useful in other ways – ways that are *equally valuable* –

Paula   The rugby coach says you've become quite an . . . 'asset'.

Edward   That's very nice of him.

Paula   Although I'm more impressed with the effect it's had on your son.

Edward   Yes.

Paula   He was walking a very fine line previously. He seemed like one of those boys, who . . .

Edward   What?

Paula   Who wasn't going to make it.

Silence.

Edward   I just need some time, okay? I'll honour my obligations I'll put things right I'm one of the few who . . . Never mind rugby, do you know what I do? I work for the government fighting to try to . . . *do good work* while my co-workers stand around, half of them waiting for their probationary period to end so they can start dropping sprogs / with –

Paula   I'm sorry, what are you saying?

Edward   What am I saying I'm a good guy that's what I'm saying.

Paula   You're a good guy.

Edward   *Yes.*

Paula   And you want *us* to support that financially? Are you asking for charity, for being 'a good guy'?

Beat.

Paula   I'm sorry but I don't see why we should support this instead of some poor immigrant from South London – we have two a year now we fund at this school, and now you're / asking us to save –

Edward   Who funds those kids?

Paula   Who do you think? . . . And some of those givers still have children in the school. They *pay* their fees on time and then I'm out there chasing them down, asking them for even more money.

Edward   I am a coach.

Paula   And we appreciate that – When is your wife arriving?

Edward   She's not coming.

Paula   But I asked to meet both of you. Your email said –

Edward   Yeah I didn't actually tell her.

Paula   But you said –

Edward   I didn't have the heart to.

Beat.

We've just got to find a way forward here. Because I can /
make all the payments.

Paula   *I* really want to make a compromise with you – and
your wife, okay? I want the school to honour Harry at the end
of term. That will be good for him. That will show his
progress. That will give him confidence. And then I will let
staff and faculty know that he and his sister will not be
returning after the holiday.

Edward   That is not – I'll sell my house.

Paula   And how many years will that fund for two children?
They are thirteen and eleven.

Beat.

Paula   Keep your house, all right? I've been here before with
too many families. You need more than just a plaster, or short-
term solution –

Edward   I have a father-in-law who can help.

Paula   But will he provide a legal guarantee for the rest of
their education? With two children you're probably talking
about a quarter of a million pounds.

Edward   So your fees are going up next year? And the year
after?

No response.

You're going to end up with a bunch of Chinese and Russian
kids. A bunch of Arabs.

Paula   Mr Knowles, ignoring the overt racism of that
comment, let me say that our position is and naturally will
remain the same: that the school provides a tremendous
service to families, a very important, private service in
education. And naturally there is a very high premium placed
on all that. We don't control that premium, but we won't

apologise for it either. It is just the function of a larger market. And if people don't like the state-school product, it's an issue to take up with the government, right? Not *us*.

Pause.

Paula   You work for the government: I'm asking you.

Scene Twenty-One

Edward *and* **Fen***'s garden in Acton.*

Edward *smokes a cigarette.*

In time, **Fen** *comes out.*

Fen   Hey, what you doing out here?

No response.

Smoking?

No response.

Fen   What's wrong?

Edward   I'm getting a new job.

Fen   Why?

Edward   I've just decided.

Fen   I thought you liked it there.

Edward   I reconsidered.

Fen   But why?

Edward   Because I did. Because . . .

Beat.

Fen   What's wrong?

Edward   'What's wrong?' – Everything . . . They want to send Jack to prison for one.

Fen Oh.

Edward 'Oh.' He's going to prison and it's going to ruin his life, his family's life.

Fen How awful. Poor Linda. The kids. Oh my God, but . . .

Edward But what?

Fen He did do it, didn't he?

Edward Yeah and now his scalp is going to be some kind of . . . trophy for the FRA.

Fen How terrible. How unlucky. But maybe he'll come out of it a better person.

Edward *What?*

Fen Who knows?

Edward Please don't say that. Jesus.

Fen Why?

Edward What did he do? What he was trying to compete with everyone else.

Fen Yes but there are rules –

Edward If everyone cheated on an exam and only Harry got caught, would you . . . would you want him punished?

Fen I'd want everyone punished. And that's your job now. How can you not do it?

Edward You know . . . That night they came over for dinner, Jack offered me a job. At First Brook. To get us back on our feet.

Fen He didn't offer out of kindness, you had something he wanted.

Edward I said no. I'm sorry: I wish I'd said yes.

Fen Why?

Edward *shrugs as if to say 'Why not?'*

Fen   No no –

Edward   Do you really . . . Fen – do you really want me to be a *guy*? Do you really want me to be just some *guy*? That's where I'm fucking heading.

Fen   You're not like Jack –

Edward   I am and what am I even getting out of it? Look at this place. We can't afford that school any more, who have we been kidding? Harry's almost fourteen, he won't be able to keep up with any of the things his mates are doing, he won't be able to have all the things *they* have – *no way*. Because his dad is a fucking muppet.

Fen   He'll be great.

Edward   Or fucking ostracised, out of the loop –

Fen   He's going to be just fine and so are we, we're . . . you're . . . well you're, you know . . .

Edward   What?

Fen   I like things as they are. And I like what you do.

Edward   'Like what I do'? Fen I *don't exist* now. And the thing is, I did all the hard part, all those crappy years at Lehman working day and night, never being at home and now? I'm nowhere. And everything else just carrying on. I'm missing out – it's more than missing out –

Fen   Don't, because . . . You're a father, I just love . . .

Edward   Fen I missed a payment on the infamous 'plan'.

Fen   What about the bracelet?

Edward   It worked, until the next payment –

Fen   So what do we . . . There are other – I've got rings too we could sell a *ring* . . .

Edward   Fen I missed a payment and got taken straight to the executioner's office, the head's asked us to remove them both at the end of term.

Beat.

Fen   Well then it's finally settled.

Edward   What do you mean?

Fen   They can go anywhere. There's nothing wrong with Acton.

Edward   What?!

Fen   You went to a normal school and *you* were fine.

Edward   'Normal'?

Beat.

I'm getting a new job. I told you. That's it, okay?

Fen   But *where*? / In the City?

Edward   In the City.

Fen   How?

Edward   I'll write my resignation letter right / now –

Fen   But why? If you go back to the City . . .

Edward   We won't have to fucking worry?

Fen   I'll never see you, for one. *I* like your job. You're *happier* – you're a coach.

Edward   Yeah – it might be like that for a while but I'm not talking about staying in the City for ever, okay?

Fen   You'll never be around again.

Edward *motions 'around' him.*

Edward   Are you saying there's a choice?

Fen   We can sell the house –

Edward   And then?

Fen   I don't know. We can live frugally.

Edward   Do you really want to live in London without me being in finance? This fucking head telling me *my* kids have to leave? *She's* going to fucking tell me and make decisions for *me*? When I can fix this?

Fen   There are other ways –

Edward   You want to move *out* of London? – It's a third-world country, *nothing is happening* out there, trust me, and I'm not talking about some house in Norfolk where people go five weeks a year to go swimming and talk about fucking birds, I'm talking about reality.

Fen   *Stay* in the government – you keep saying the City's over. 'It's finished.' 'It's going down.'

Edward   Then loot the sinking ship. Because if it goes down and we don't have anything we're done for. And if it doesn't go down we'll be fine – more than fine. And really, the whole thing doesn't have to last for ever, if the whole system can just last . . . five more years, that will be enough. So just let me go back, five years in the City, okay?

Fen   I don't –

Edward   Five years. In five years – no in *two* – I can go to that school and shit on the head's desk and she won't be able to say a damn thing. I'll be supporting her fucking immigrants.

Fen   What?

Edward   *Five years*, okay? Everything only has to last five more years.

Fen   Yeah, then what?

Edward   Then we'll be safe – if it all comes down it won't really matter. We'll be okay. Fuck the rest of it. No one else matters. We'll be safe with some basic dignity. And I can tell that bitch to get fucked.

Pause.

Fen   What an awful thing to say.

Edward   Never mind – we can still make a killing. What I'm saying is we can do it, okay?

Fen *shakes her head 'No', but* **Edward** *has already turned away from her and can't see it.*

Edward   I'll write my resignation letter right now, I can't wait to throw it in my boss's face as soon as possible. He wants me to fuck about with paper clips in some office with a smile on my face, *fuck him*. But there's just one thing I've got to take care of first. I've got to do something to make all this right.

Scene Twenty-Two

Sir Roger*'s office, First Brook Capital.*

Sir Roger, **Kim** *and* **Emma**.

Sir Roger   You think I care? Jack is going to jail, so this guy can fuck off. Throw him out.

Emma   I really don't think I can. He wants to talk to / you.

Sir Roger   And why's that?

Emma   I don't know.

Sir Roger   He probably wants to gloat about the conviction – I won't give him the pleasure.

Kim   It's our swaps, I know it.

Sir Roger   That's perfectly legal and I won't have our name dragged through the mud any more. If he thinks he can turn a tanker around with a dinghy, he's mistaken.

Emma   He's quite adamant.

Sir Roger   I'm busy.

Emma   He knows you're here.

Sir Roger   How does he know I'm here?

Emma   I don't know.

Kim   Send him in.

Sir Roger   Why?

Kim   Be smart please.

Sir Roger   Okay okay fine. Send him in.

Emma *leaves.*

Edward *enters.* **Sir Roger** *shakes hands with him.*

Sir Roger   Hello. Roger Glynn and this is Kim Lopez.

Edward *and* **Kim** *shake hands, 'Hi', 'Hello' etc*

Sir Roger   Sit down – if you like?

Edward *sits.*

Sir Roger   How can we be of service?

Kim   Do I . . . know you?

Edward   Excuse me?

Kim   Do I know you? I never forget / a –

Edward (*to* **Sir Roger**)   I'm here about your credit default swaps.

Sir Roger   Am I being investigated? It's very kind of you to come see me, but I did nothing wrong. Read the rulebook. I have huge brand with the Financial Regulations Authority and I'll fight to protect it. They think the sun shines out of my arse.

Edward   Be that as it may, you've got a problem.

Sir Roger   I don't have a problem. And after that whole Jack Tilly fiasco, I'm not going to have *another* problem.

Edward   You're still making money. Not many people can say that.

Sir Roger   So I sold some swaps to my old bank. Who cares.

Edward   Because it's a glaring conflict of interest. You made huge profits by selling products from one company that you're a part of to another company you're a part of.

Sir Roger   I'm a part of *one* company: First Brook Capital.

Edward   You're part of RNBS as well.

Sir Roger   I left years ago. What's wrong with you people? I *left* that bank to start First Brook. I have nothing to do with RNBS and haven't for ages.

Edward   I know. But you still have a certain number of unredeemed stock options at your old bank, options that you never cashed in – and they're still there. Waiting for you, down at RNBS.

Sir Roger   There's no such thing. I *left*. And when I did I cashed all my options *out*. I'll send you the paperwork.

Edward   You missed your first two years.

Sir Roger   You're insane.

Edward   '92, '93.

Edward *throws a file onto the table.* **Sir Roger** *picks it up and looks at it. He is horrified by what he reads.*

Kim   (*finally recognising* **Edward**) *Starbucks guy*, oh my God you're Starbucks guy.

Edward   (*to Sir Roger:*) Some of your bonus was in stock options. You didn't get much, I don't blame you for forgetting about them – you went on to such grand things. I doubt even you can keep track of your wealth, in all its forms. But I know you forgot about those old stock options. Because you never cashed them in. They're still on the books at RNBS, unrestricted, unredeemed.

Kim   Roger?

Edward   As RNBS has now been taken over by the government, those stocks are now worth almost nothing . . . but they're still yours, of course. So when you started that little money carousel with Ms Lopez, they qualified you for a very illegal conflict of interests.

Kim   *Roger?*

Edward   On the heels of Jack Tilly, it will surely bring First Brook down. At least. But look on the bright side, at least you've still got the stock options, nice one. You ought to cash them in. Maybe you can buy lunch with the proceeds . . . a sandwich at Pret. Actually, maybe only half a sandwich.

Sir Roger   Yes, well, thank you for coming to visit.

Edward   Is that it?

Sir Roger   I'll need to conference with my own parties to –

Edward   Sure, sure . . . make sure they see all that while you're doing it.

Sir Roger (*overlooking the documents*)   I will, thank you.

Edward   Of course, the FRA doesn't know about this yet, and I really don't want to tell them.

Pause.

Sir Roger   Why not?

Kim   You don't want to tell them?

Edward   No. I want a job.

Sir Roger   Excuse me?

Edward   I'd like to come work as a partner at your fund, represent First Brook on industry groups. Maybe be more of a generalist. It's not an uncommon jump.

Sir Roger   And you'll bury this?

Edward   Irrevocably.

Pause.

Sir Roger   Well . . . is this a problem, *really*, or an opportunity? I can see… I can *imagine* you coming aboard in a . . . capacity. (*To* **Kim**.) Right?

Kim   Certainly, sure . . . I'm so glad you came to see us.

Edward *gives* **Kim** *a look.*

Edward   May I speak to Sir Roger alone please?

Kim   Why?

Edward   I'd just like to have a word with Sir Roger alone.

Kim *doesn't move.*

Sir Roger   *Go*, will you?

Kim *goes to exit, but then stops.*

Kim   No, sorry. Anything you say to him can be said to me.

Beat. **Sir Roger** *shrugs.*

Sir Roger (*to* **Edward***)*   Go ahead, it's fine. I promise you.

Edward   . . . I've got one hard condition of employment.

Sir Roger   What is it?

Edward   She works for me.

Scene Twenty-Three

Starbucks.

Edward *enters and approaches the counter. There is no one there. He looks over the counter and spots someone offstage.*

Edward (*to someone offstage*)   Hey EXCUSE ME – hello? You got a *customer*?

Andrzej *enters from behind the counter. He breaks into a forced smile.*

Edward   'COFFEE', please?

Andrzej   Yes. What coffee?

Edward *takes a £20 note out of his wallet.*

Edward   *Black* coffee.

Andrzej   I know you . . .

Edward (*ignoring this*)   And keep that twenty as a tip please.

Andrzej's *smile turns genuine as he takes the money.*

Andrzej   Thank you much. Wow.

He admires the note, then looks back up at **Edward**.

Andrzej   Okay, what size black coffee?

Edward   The normal.

Andrzej (*unsure what this means*)   'Normal' . . . okay . . .

Edward *peruses the menu.*

Edward   Actually . . . scratch the coffee.

Andrzej   'Scratch the coffee'?

Edward   Yeah. Forget it.

Andrzej *deliberates on whether or not to hand back the money, but as soon as he holds it back out to* **Edward** –

Edward   I think what I'd actually like is a . . .

Andrzej *keeps the note, happily.*

Andrzej   / Yes?

Edward   Grande half-skinny half-one per cent extra hot split triple shot latte with whip.

Beat.

Andrzej   O/kay –

Edward   And can I get that with an extra shot of full caff? Ta.

He checks his phone. **Andrzej** *hesitates.*

Andrzej   Can I / ask –

Edward   And I'm in 'a rush'? Hence the tip . . .

Andrzej *sheepishly disappears while* **Edward** *buries himself in his phone.*

In time, **Linda** *enters from the side. She has a Starbucks mug and pulls her pram behind her.*

Linda   Edward.

Edward   Oh – hi. Hi.

Linda   Does your phone not work or something?

She notices he's using it.

I was about ready to come over to your bloody house in Acton – what happened?

Beat.

What *happened*?

Edward   I'm sorry, okay? Really sor/ry –

Linda   You promised him / you'd –

Edward   What can I do? Didn't I quit my job over it? I quit because what they did to him it isn't fair you're right but that's it –

Linda   Isn't there anything you can do about it? I can't let him – Isn't there something you can do?

Edward   What do you mean?

Linda   To get him downgraded to a better prison at least?

Edward   I don't / know.

Linda   Is there anyone you can ask?

Edward   Where?

Linda   The *FRA*?

Edward   / Christ.

Linda   You must know someone at the FRA? We need a –

Edward   / No.

Linda   We need just a connection, some kind of appeal –

Edward   I'm not friendly with that lot –

Linda   *I'll* approach / them –

Edward   I stormed out! Because of Jack!

Linda   And went straight to First Brook. You had a connection there. My husband. You owe us.

Edward   He had nothing to do with it.

Linda   Then how did you end up going to the / one –

Edward   The City is a small place, there aren't many places to go. It was just an unhappy coincidence. They were hiring.

His text message goes off in his hand. He checks it.

(*Reading.*) And I've got a meeting to . . . I'm sorry.

Linda   Can't we get First Brook's help?

Edward   Why?

Linda   Maybe they could . . . pay the fine from the FRA?

Edward   No they can't.

Linda   He *worked* there. Shouldn't they?

Edward   I just don't think . . . there's money for / that.

Linda   Will they pay part of it?

Edward   No.

Linda   Can't Sir Roger talk to someone?

Edward   They've told you Linda, they can't help you.

Andrzej *appears with the coffee and hands it to* **Jack**. *It is in a takeaway cup.*

Edward (*to* **Andrzej**)   Can I get this to take away please?

Linda   I'm just trying to make it better.

Andrzej   Yes, is takeaway.

Edward *realises this but gives* **Andrzej** *a look anyway. He tastes the coffee, then hands it back.*

Edward   This is wrong.

Andrzej   Yes . . . can you repeat order?

Edward   I don't have time – just give me my money back.

Andrzej   I can –

Edward   You screwed up. I want my money back.

Beat. **Andrzej** *exits.*

Linda   Tell me what I can do? I don't know how . . .

Edward   What about your / father –

Linda   My father's working on it, he said there's someone he knew at school who's a judge but . . . he can't even remember if they were *friends.* And I'm up all night hoping they were, that they were friends fifty years ago. I'm going crazy thinking about all the different ways they could have been friends . . . that this *judge* might remember my dad and . . .

Edward   Can I find you a better lawyer, to –

Linda   To what?

Edward   I don't know.

Linda *starts to cry.*

Linda   We've got nothing coming in to pay for one now anyway.

Edward   Right.

Linda   My father's paying our mortgage until we sell. We have to sell to pay the FRA –

Edward   Yeah. I saw your place on a property website.

Linda *is beyond embarrassed.*

Edward (*looking around, lowering his voice to a whisper*)   It's not a scandal, it's not gossip, no one was talking about it. It was just that Fen and I were looking around. We were curious. About the prices around here . . . Who isn't?

Linda   Edward can you help me?

Andrzej *returns and gives* **Edward** *his twenty pounds back.*

Edward   I want to –

Linda   WE NEED MONEY.

Edward   What can I . . .

Andrzej *freezes, then walks quietly away.*

Linda   I always tried to help you, when you were . . . (*She looks around.*) *HERE*, right?

Edward   Yeah I know I appreciated that. Very much. Didn't I?

Linda   Not even my father knows what to do, or even what to *say*. That's the worst part. He's never known anyone . . . who went to prison.

She cries.

He's never known anyone like *us*.

Edward   It's okay. It's okay.

Linda   What the fuck am I going to do?! I need money and I need a *husband* –

Edward   He'll get out. In a little while.

Linda   Three years and eight months.

Edward   Things will get better.

Linda   I lie in bed at night and think, 'This must be what divorce feels like, when you've got a baby and two small boys, and you're all alone, and you're stuck.' But then I remember Jack's in prison, that he's not dead and he hasn't left me, and I don't know if I feel relieved or even worse.

Edward   I really am sorry.

Linda   My mother suggested a divorce. She never liked Jack it was like . . . she knew all along. And she's upset about everything yes she cares I know she does but there was still this . . . triumph.

Edward   She just doesn't want her daughter married to a −

He stops himself.

Linda   I don't know anyone who's got divorced. No one from school, no one from uni, I hate the idea. Jack is my husband but when I look forward . . . who are we?

Edward   Let me just buy you a quick coffee before I go. What would you like?

Linda   Well, another skinny latte please.

Edward (*to* **Andrzej**)   Skinny latte.

Andrzej   What size?

Edward (*surprisingly aggressive*)   The biggest, okay? Just *get it.*

Andrzej *scurries off.*

Linda   Do you think I could get a job at least? I went to Bristol. I've got a degree.

Edward   In Archaeology Studies.

Linda   And I never really did any work

Edward   I'd like to get you some money Linda.

Beat.

Linda   Thank you.

Edward   No worries. (*He exhales deeply.*) You came running over, I was worried. I thought it was about your house.

Linda   I know, I'm so mortified being on property websites . . .

Edward   Yeah and it's not like houses like yours come up very often. Not in Fulham anyway.

Linda   That's why I come here all day, I have to be out while people fucking 'view'.

Edward   And . . . like I said: I'm looking for a house. With Fen.

Linda   You said.

Edward   So we saw yours online –

Pause.

Linda   You're not . . .

Edward   I went around looking at some places with the estate agent – listen no it was quite innocent – and walking down your street, it took me about ten seconds to put together that we were going to look at *your* house –

Linda   You went *inside*?

Edward   Well I didn't want to be *rude*. I couldn't be. This was my estate agent –

Linda   In my house?

Edward (*ignoring this*)   I think he's being a little too aggressive though – prices aren't *that high,* even for a house like that one.

Linda   What's wrong with you? Have you no –

Edward   I could solve a lot of your problems. It would be weird of course it would be weird but you could be sure of a good price, and that your buyer wouldn't bugger up a sale at the last second and leave you high and dry . . .

Linda   *No.*

Edward   Don't you see? You sell it at a high price, higher than it deserves. *I'm* just dying to get out of Acton. I'll pay a premium for that if it's to get into the right house. And then both sides will win. I'll be doing you a great favour.

No response.

It was just an idea.

Beat.

Linda *physically attacks* **Edward**. *'You bastard', 'You utter bastard' etc.*

Andrzej *rushes on to the scene and tries to prise* **Linda** *away from* **Edward**, *but she's determined.*

Scene Twenty-Four

Prison.

Jack *sits at a table in his (white-collar) prison clothes.* **Edward** *sits across from him.* **Edward**'s *posh shirt mirrors the colour of* **Jack**'s *uniform.*

Edward   How's the food?

No response.

Not good, huh?

No response.

Do they really let you play cricket?

No response.

Mmm . . .

No response.

You going to talk to me? You came in the room.

Jack   I just wanted to get out of my cell.

Edward   Oh.

Jack   So thanks for that.

Edward   Yeah, umm. I need to –

Jack   I was hoping you'd let me sit in peace.

Edward   I drove all the way up here.

Jack *puts his head in his hands with tired frustration.*

Edward   I need to talk to you. It's your wife. She's lost it. She won't leave us alone. She's everywhere . . . it's awful.

Jack *looks at* **Edward***.*

Edward   Not for me, it's not about me, it's about Fen, and the kids. It's becoming like torture for them.

No response.

Linda . . . she's even going for little Kathy – Kathy went to a birthday party in Fulham and it was a disaster, she can't go to riding school now because of the pony club mothers . . . Now it's starting in school, it's like all the mothers have . . .

No response.

Please I want you to . . . I want you to tell Linda to stop.

No response.

You've got to make her stop. You've got to talk some sense into her.

No response.

I need you to talk to her.

Jack   Talk to her.

Edward   Yes.

Jack   I'm incarcerated.

Edward   I'm sure / it's –

Jack   And you're going to come in here and tell me what to do, how my *family* should –

Edward   It's / about –

Jack   If my wife finds some stress relief in telling your family what a lying decrepit sack of shit you are, then good –

Edward   When did I lie?

Beat.

It's not my fault.

Jack   Whose fault is it?

Edward   The FRA, the *government* I told you.

Jack   You *told* me that – just before you said you were moving on to First Brook.

Edward   You're the one who said I'd fit in well there.

Jack   I told you they were crooks! And now Linda tells me you were asking about our fucking *house*.

Edward   It was just an idea.

Pause.

Let's not . . . What's done is done. On *all* sides.

Jack *pushes out of his chair and stands up.*

Jack   Sanctimonious prick.

Edward   I tried!

Jack   And?

Edward   And . . . Come on, my little daughter, you went to her christening. She doesn't deserve this. The *hostility* that's been –

Jack   My wife can do whatever she wants Edward, as long as it's within the letter of the law. And there's not a damn thing you can / do about it.

Edward   Kathy doesn't deserve –

Jack   *Linda* doesn't deserve to be out there without a husband. They come in here at the weekend, I try to talk to my kids, who are *ashamed*, I try to console my wife and I talk about when the house will sell! And why? To be a national example for what is basically the fucking common law?! We've exported it everywhere, everyone agrees and *I'm* getting fucked? *Here?!*

He looks around awkwardly. Someone is staring at him.

(*To distant prison guard.*) *Sorry*, I'm fine, yes just a little chat, sorry I'll . . .

He sits down and tries to appear calm.

Edward   I came because of my family. Tell Linda that she can mobilise all of West London against *me* but not my family. Kathy's scared and lonely now. She comes home from school and thinks everyone hates her and she asks why . . . She's lost her appetite, Fen just cries . . .

Pause.

Jack   How cold-blooded are you?

Pause. An offstage security guard gets **Jack**'s *attention.*

Jack (*to offstage guard*)   Yeah . . . okay. (*To* **Edward**.) Wonderful seeing a mate.

He stands up. **Edward** *slowly stands up.*

Edward   Is there anything . . . ?

Jack   No. You don't have anything I want, so you can't make a deal. Tough.

Edward   Yeah, I guess you're right . . . And I'm sorry. I'm really sorry.

He starts to leave. **Jack** *watches.*

Edward *turns back, as if to say something, then storms off.*

Jack *smiles. He turns back towards the security guard in triumph.*

Scene Twenty-Five

Posh restaurant.

Sir Roger, **Edward** *and* **Fen**.

Edward *is showing* **Sir Roger** *a shirt voucher.*

Edward   So you take it to any of their stores and get twenty-five per cent off.

Sir Roger   Wow, I love their shirts – but why are they using . . .

He waves the voucher.

Edward   Everyone is now. The recession.

Sir Roger   Then that's great. If everyone is doing it.

He downs his drink.

Must be off. Nice seeing you.

Fen   You too.

Sir Roger   Where's that house, between the Palace Road and the river?

Edward   Yes.

Sir Roger   I hope they accept your bid.

Edward   So do we.

Sir Roger (*to* **Fen**)   You must be very excited.

He kisses **Fen**.

Fen   It's an exciting time.

Sir Roger   Yeah, I should go work for the FRA for a while, does wonders for your career.

He and **Edward** *laugh.*

Edward   You never get angry at me for all that?

Sir Roger   We buried the hatchet, didn't we?

Edward   Of course it's just –

Sir Roger   Don't say anything more. Now we've got to forget that the hatchet is there. That's the real trick in relationships.

Fen   Yes.

Sir Roger   Anyway, I hope you get it.

He raises his glass, **Edward** *and* **Fen** *follow suit.*

Sir Roger *notices his glass is empty.*

Sir Roger   Ah shame, ah well: pleasure as always.

Edward   Likewise Roger.

Sir Roger   And thank you for this . . .

Edward   Voucher.

Sir Roger   I can't wait to use it, what excellent value . . .

Edward   Absolutely.

Sir Roger   To infinity and beyond.

He wanders off staring at the voucher and muttering about 'value'.

Fen   It destroys your soul to see someone that wealthy getting excited about a shirt voucher.

Edward   Don't worry, it's out of date.

Fen   The man is a menace.

Edward *puts his phone on the table and stares at it.*

Edward   Are you excited? Maybe we've *done it*.

He kisses her.

They'll call and – don't you think there's something *triumphant* about going back to Fulham?

He leans over and kisses **Fen***, then raises his glass.*

Fen   I don't want to go back.

Edward   What? *Why?* We'll take care of Linda.

Fen   I don't care what Linda does.

Edward   Then what are you talking about? We put in a bid. *You* put in a bid.

Fen   I can't stomach it.

Edward   You've had too much to drink, that's / all.

Fen   I've been wanting to talk about it, but you're never around.

Edward   What's the problem?

Fen   I can't stand it.

Edward   Is it your friends?

Fen   My friends?

Edward   They'll take you back, you'll be close to them again it was just like a little holiday we took . . . in Acton.

Fen   I don't have 'friends' there, you *go* places – cafés, the park, a dinner party.

Edward   It's called making an effort.

Fen   I went back there last week for lunch with Caroline and her sister.

Edward   Really?

Fen   Just to see if I could do it.

Edward   It will take some time to re-acclimatise, that's all –

Fen   You know how many conversations started with 'I was reading somewhere . . . '? About things they would never . . . 'I was reading somewhere that stairs are good for you', 'I was reading that Leeds is one of the happiest places in Britain'. Then we talked about Beirut. I wanted to scream, run through one of the windows and then fall two floors to my death. Give them a shock. Something right in front of them . . . But I knew they'd just look down at my corpse and say 'She's one of those'.

Edward   You're losing it – Acton is not some Glaswegian estate, it's fucking *Acton*, what do they talk about?

Fen   Things they have *to do*.

Edward   I don't get this – first you don't want to leave and now –

Fen   Edward I've decided I'm not moving back to Fulham. It's final.

Edward   So I've spent the past few months in the business class of some jet, that's no reason to go crazy. I did it for today, so we could wait for *this phone call*. So we can get the *house*.

No response.

So we can have another child.

Beat.

Fen   What?

Edward   What I really want to do is make a baby.

Fen   Eddie . . .

Edward   I think we should go for it.

Fen   I don't love you any more.

Pause.

Edward   But I'm doing this for you – for the *family*. Why do you think I work so hard? I'm back in the top one per cent because I want what's best for my family. What does that say about the ninety-nine per cent?

Beat.

Edward   This was all about your happiness.

Fen   *I* take care of my kids, and my happiness. I would have loved to have taken care of you, but I can't.

Silence.

Edward   I'm not going to miss this chance. Not now. We *need* this – I finally figured out all the numbers on the combination lock, don't you see? And no one told me, *I* fucking did it myself, you know, it's taken for ever. I'm not walking away now.

Fen   I'm leaving.

Edward   Fine. You want to leave? Leave.

His mobile rings. He does not answer it. It continues to ring over the following.

Fen   And I'm taking the kids.

Edward   You can't.

Fen   I'm keeping them out –

Edward   I said you *can't*. Think about it –

Fen   Are you going to take care of them? You'd have to work less.

Edward   You're serious.

Pause.

Fine. You want to try to run things? Well I'm in control, so I'll price this up like a trade: *I'm keeping control.*

The signal goes off for a new voicemail.

Fen   You should check it.

Edward *checks the message.*

Fen   Did they accept the bid?

Edward   Yes.

Scene Twenty-Six

Sir Roger*'s office, First Brook.*

Emma *is in tears.* **Edward** *and* **Kim** *watch* **Emma** *try to pull herself together. Everyone wears black.*

Emma   Sorry.

She stands up straight, puts her brave face on.

The turnout was very impressive, don't you think?

Kim   Yes.

Edward   Yes I was relieved. Investors can't show up at Roger's funeral and then pull their money out, not in the same week anyway. We've bought some time –

Emma   What I mean is, they paid their respects.

Pause.

Didn't they?

Edward   Yes.

Kim   It was a beautiful service.

Emma   It was nice to see his family there.

Edward   Which one?

Beat.

Emma   His first wife, and their children. I haven't seen them all together in years.

Kim   We should send them flowers.

Emma   I was already thinking about it in the car. (*To* **Edward**.) Would you like to write a note?

Edward   Could you put one in for me.

Emma   And what should I say?

Edward   I'm 'shocked and saddened' by Roger's death.

Emma, *a bit disappointed, turns to* **Kim**, *who suddenly looks nervous.*

Kim   Oh, I don't know . . . That, that was my first funeral to be honest.

Edward *gives a nasty laugh.*

Kim   Can you . . . I don't know . . . tell them I'm hugely saddened.

Beat.

Emma   Okay.

She goes to leave, but turns at the door.

Oh, I also need to email the papers.

Edward   Don't they have their own obituary writers? Are they asking us to do it for free?

Emma   No. They want a statement from us about Occupy London.

Beat.

Edward   What did Roger say for this kind of thing?

Emma   I was going to . . . Well, should I just say something about them being just rather silly, not doing any good and it's borderline mad –

Edward   What? You can't say that.

Emma (*impatient*)   Fine – what would you like to say?

Beat.

Edward   'The Occupy actions lack stringent aims and sometimes feature elements of event culture.'

Beat.

Emma   That's actually quite good.

Edward   Thank you.

She leaves. **Edward** *turns to* **Kim**, *all business.*

Edward   Has that deal gone through?

Kim   It's not –

Edward   I don't care what lawyers you've got to bring in, for fuck's sake sort it out.

Kim   The / court may not –

Edward   Why are you telling me this? Tell a lawyer. I want that sale at the agreed price and fuck everyone else.

Kim   Okay okay.

Edward   Okay what?

Kim   I'll do it.

Edward   *Go.* You're asleep at the wheel.

Beat. **Kim** *doesn't move.*

Edward   *Now.* And don't fucking mention Greece to me again today! I don't want to hear any more about it!

Kim *doesn't move.*

Kim   I don't know if this is the right time to tell you, but . . .

Edward   What?

Kim   I'm uh, I'm leaving. I'm giving notice. Now.

Edward   What? You can't, you'll miss your bonus. You're only a few months away.

Kim   I know but . . . I think I've lost my relevance here.

Edward   Yes, well I could have told you that.

Kim   You did.

Beat.

Edward   You sure? That money will go back into the bonus pool for everyone else.

Kim   I'm sure. I want to leave.

Edward   Then I wish you the best of luck. Now go take care of that shit for me before you leave today.

Kim *exits.*

Emma *buzzes.*

Emma (*voice*)   Your two o'clock is here.

Edward   Send him in.

Emma *shows* **Chris** *in, then exits.*

Edward   Chris.

Chris   How are you?

They shake hands.

Edward   You?

Chris   Fine.

He sits. **Edward** *leans up against the desk.*

Chris   Thanks for meeting with me.

Edward   What's wrong?

Chris *laughs, nervously.*

Chris   Nothing's *wrong*. Except Sir Roger – I'm very sorry. My deepest condolences.

Edward   Thank you yes, it is a time of grieving. We're all deeply . . . saddened.

Chris   I'm sure.

Edward   And how are you? Busy?

Chris   Yeah, I guess.

Silence.

Edward   Is the FRA looking into anything –

Chris   No no, why would you think that?

Edward   I left. I'm making some money. I figured I was a prime target.

Chris   No. No no no.

Edward   Well . . . you're *here.*

Chris   We think the world of you. Besides, Henry has bigger things to worry about.

Edward   Is he okay?

Chris   They're dissolving the FRA. It's official.

Edward   I'm sorry to hear that. Not generally . . . but it must put you in a difficult position . . . your career.

Chris   All that power is going to the Bank of England –

Edward   I heard. Cameron loves to rearrange deckchairs.

Chris   Yeah, well . . .

Edward   I hope you get a better boss there, anyway.

Chris   That's the thing, I don't know. It's an uncertain time.

Edward   Sure. First Brook's thinking of moving overseas.

Chris   Where?

Edward   We're looking at a few places. The climate here . . . it's becoming very anti-success.

Chris   That's why I wanted to meet with you actually . . . to talk about First Brook.

Edward   Okay.

Chris   I want to ask you for a job.

Edward   Oh.

Chris   I brought you my CV.

Edward   You don't have to bring me your CV.

Beat.

Edward   If I hear of anything –

Chris   You don't have any more vacancies?

Edward   No.

Chris   Mate, I've got a son, a mortgage.

Edward *nods gravely, professing huge sadness.*

Edward   I wish you the best of all possible luck.

Chris   Thank you.

Edward   I'm actually late and have to go.

Chris   Is there anything / at –

Edward   No.

Chris   Have you heard of anything anywhere else?

Edward   No.

Chris   Why do I think you're not telling the truth?

Edward   There you go, always suspicious.

Chris   No no, it's not that. I just . . .

Beat.

Edward   It's nothing personal.

Pause.

Honestly.

Chris   I believe you.

Edward   But let me . . . let me tell you something I learned in my Lehman days, something you should keep in mind: it takes a certain kind of person to work in the City. A competitive person, and the system works because a small fraction of the population wants to compete, and they succeed. They're the world's engines. They're the ones who make things work. They provide the quality.

Beat.

And you're not a quality person.

Chris *looks at* **Edward** *with no cards to play, and leaves.*

Edward *walks towards* **Sir Roger**'*s desk smiling to himself.*

He takes a good look at the desk, and then he sits down at it, like a new king getting on the throne for the first time.

He sits there powerfully for few seconds.

Then **Emma** *enters carrying a stack of new shirts. She begins laying them out on the table for him to choose from.*

Edward *watches her with a smile.*

References

Sir Mervin King - Treasury Committee - Bank of England - July 2012 - Fixing LIBOR: Some Preliminary Findings – © Parliamentary copyright 2012

http://www.publications.parliament.uk/pa/cm201213/cmselect/cmtreasy/481/48108.htm#note281

Lord Turner – Treasury Committee – Bank of England – June 2012 – Financial Stability Report –Minutes of Evidence – © Parliamentary copyright 2012

http://www.publications.parliament.uk/pa/cm201213/cmselect/cmtreasy/535/120717.htm

Andrew Feldstein. Source:

http://www.cnbc.com/id/48445134/Hedge_Funds_Rail_on_Markets_Regulators

Barclays manager to the FSA regarding LIBOR. Source:

http://www.economist.com/node/21558281

Methuen Drama Modern Plays

include work by

Edward Albee
Jean Anouilh
John Arden
Margaretta D'Arcy
Peter Barnes
Sebastian Barry
Brendan Behan
Dermot Bolger
Edward Bond
Bertolt Brecht
Howard Brenton
Anthony Burgess
Simon Burke
Jim Cartwright
Caryl Churchill
Complicite
Noël Coward
Lucinda Coxon
Sarah Daniels
Nick Darke
Nick Dear
Shelagh Delaney
David Edgar
David Eldridge
Dario Fo
Michael Frayn
John Godber
Paul Godfrey
David Greig
John Guare
Peter Handke
David Harrower
Jonathan Harvey
Iain Heggie
Declan Hughes
Terry Johnson
Sarah Kane
Charlotte Keatley
Barrie Keeffe

Howard Korder
Robert Lepage
Doug Lucie
Martin McDonagh
John McGrath
Terrence McNally
David Mamet
Patrick Marber
Arthur Miller
Mtwa, Ngema & Simon
Tom Murphy
Phyllis Nagy
Peter Nichols
Sean O'Brien
Joseph O'Connor
Joe Orton
Louise Page
Joe Penhall
Luigi Pirandello
Stephen Poliakoff
Franca Rame
Mark Ravenhill
Philip Ridley
Reginald Rose
Willy Russell
Jean-Paul Sartre
Sam Shepard
Wole Soyinka
Simon Stephens
Shelagh Stephenson
Peter Straughan
C. P. Taylor
Theatre Workshop
Sue Townsend
Judy Upton
Timberlake Wertenbaker
Roy Williams
Snoo Wilson
Victoria Wood

Methuen Drama Contemporary Dramatists

include

John Arden (two volumes)
Arden & D'Arcy
Peter Barnes (three volumes)
Sebastian Barry
Dermot Bolger
Edward Bond (eight volumes)
Howard Brenton
  (two volumes)
Richard Cameron
Jim Cartwright
Caryl Churchill (two volumes)
Sarah Daniels (two volumes)
Nick Darke
David Edgar (three volumes)
David Eldridge
Ben Elton
Dario Fo (two volumes)
Michael Frayn (three volumes)
David Greig
John Godber (four volumes)
Paul Godfrey
John Guare
Lee Hall (two volumes)
Peter Handke
Jonathan Harvey
  (two volumes)
Declan Hughes
Terry Johnson (three volumes)
Sarah Kane
Barrie Keeffe
Bernard-Marie Koltès
  (two volumes)
Franz Xaver Kroetz
David Lan
Bryony Lavery
Deborah Levy
Doug Lucie

David Mamet (four volumes)
Martin McDonagh
Duncan McLean
Anthony Minghella
  (two volumes)
Tom Murphy (six volumes)
Phyllis Nagy
Anthony Neilsen (two volumes)
Philip Osment
Gary Owen
Louise Page
Stewart Parker (two volumes)
Joe Penhall (two volumes)
Stephen Poliakoff
  (three volumes)
David Rabe (two volumes)
Mark Ravenhill (two volumes)
Christina Reid
Philip Ridley
Willy Russell
Eric-Emmanuel Schmitt
Ntozake Shange
Sam Shepard (two volumes)
Wole Soyinka (two volumes)
Simon Stephens (two volumes)
Shelagh Stephenson
David Storey (three volumes)
Sue Townsend
Judy Upton
Michel Vinaver
  (two volumes)
Arnold Wesker (two volumes)
Michael Wilcox
Roy Williams (three volumes)
Snoo Wilson (two volumes)
David Wood (two volumes)
Victoria Wood

Methuen Drama Modern Classics

Jean Anouilh *Antigone* • Brendan Behan *The Hostage* • Robert Bolt *A Man for All Seasons* • Edward Bond *Saved* • Bertolt Brecht *The Caucasian Chalk Circle* • *Fear and Misery in the Third Reich* • *The Good Person of Szechwan* • *Life of Galileo* • *The Messingkauf Dialogues* • *Mother Courage and Her Children* • *Mr Puntila and His Man Matti* • *The Resistible Rise of Arturo Ui* • *Rise and Fall of the City of Mahagonny* • *The Threepenny Opera* • Jim Cartwright *Road* • *Two & Bed* • Caryl Churchill *Serious Money* • *Top Girls* • Noël Coward *Blithe Spirit* • *Hay Fever* • *Present Laughter* • *Private Lives* • *The Vortex* • Shelagh Delaney *A Taste of Honey* • Dario Fo *Accidental Death of an Anarchist* • Michael Frayn *Copenhagen* • Lorraine Hansberry *A Raisin in the Sun* • Jonathan Harvey *Beautiful Thing* • David Mamet *Glengarry Glen Ross* • *Oleanna* • *Speed-the-Plow* • Patrick Marber *Closer* • *Dealer's Choice* • Arthur Miller *Broken Glass* • Percy Mtwa, Mbongeni Ngema, Barney Simon *Woza Albert!* • Joe Orton *Entertaining Mr Sloane* • *Loot* • *What the Butler Saw* • Mark Ravenhill *Shopping and F***ing* • Willy Russell *Blood Brothers* • *Educating Rita* • *Stags and Hens* • *Our Day Out* • Jean-Paul Sartre *Crime Passionnel* • Wole Soyinka • *Death and the King's Horseman* • Theatre Workshop *Oh, What a Lovely War* • Frank Wedekind • *Spring Awakening* • Timberlake Wertenbaker *Our Country's Good*

Methuen Drama Student Editions

Jean Anouilh *Antigone* • John Arden *Serjeant Musgrave's Dance*
Alan Ayckbourn *Confusions* • Aphra Behn *The Rover* • Edward Bond
Lear • *Saved* • Bertolt Brecht *The Caucasian Chalk Circle* • *Fear and
Misery in the Third Reich* • *The Good Person of Szechwan* • *Life of Galileo* •
Mother Courage and her Children • *The Resistible Rise of Arturo Ui* • *The
Threepenny Opera* • Anton Chekhov *The Cherry Orchard* • *The Seagull* •
Three Sisters • *Uncle Vanya* • Caryl Churchill *Serious Money* • *Top Girls*
• Shelagh Delaney *A Taste of Honey* • Euripides Elektra • *Medea* •
Dario Fo *Accidental Death of an Anarchist* • Michael Frayn *Copenhagen*
• John Galsworthy *Strife* • Nikolai Gogol *The Government Inspector* •
Robert Holman *Across Oka* • Henrik Ibsen *A Doll's House* • *Ghosts* •
Hedda Gabler • Charlotte Keatley *My Mother Said I Never Should* •
Bernard Kops *Dreams of Anne Frank* • Federico García Lorca *Blood
Wedding* • *Doña Rosita the Spinster* (bilingual edition) • *The House of
Bernarda Alba* • (bilingual edition) • *Yerma* (bilingual edition) • David
Mamet *Glengarry Glen Ross* • *Oleanna* • Patrick Marber *Closer* • John
Marston *The Malcontent* • Martin McDonagh *The Lieutenant of Inishmore* •
Joe Orton *Loot* • Luigi Pirandello *Six Characters in Search of an Author*
• Mark Ravenhill *Shopping and F***ing* • Willy Russell *Blood Brothers*
• *Educating Rita* • Sophocles *Antigone* • *Oedipus the King* • Wole
Soyinka *Death and the King's Horseman* • Shelagh Stephenson *The
Memory of Water* • August Strindberg *Miss Julie* • J. M. Synge *The
Playboy of the Western World* • Theatre Workshop *Oh What a Lovely
War* Timberlake Wertenbaker *Our Country's Good* • Arnold Wesker
The Merchant • Oscar Wilde *The Importance of Being Earnest* •
Tennessee Williams *A Streetcar Named Desire* • *The Glass Menagerie*

Methuen Drama World Classics

include

Jean Anouilh (two volumes)
Brendan Behan
Aphra Behn
Bertolt Brecht (eight volumes)
Büchner
Bulgakov
Calderón
Čapek
Anton Chekhov
Noël Coward (eight volumes)
Feydeau (two volumes)
Eduardo De Filippo
Max Frisch
John Galsworthy
Gogol
Gorky (two volumes)
Harley Granville Barker
  (two volumes)
Victor Hugo
Henrik Ibsen (six volumes)
Jarry

Lorca (three volumes)
Marivaux
Mustapha Matura
David Mercer (two volumes)
Arthur Miller (six volumes)
Molière
Musset
Peter Nichols (two volumes)
Joe Orton
A. W. Pinero
Luigi Pirandello
Terence Rattigan
  (two volumes)
W. Somerset Maugham
  (two volumes)
August Strindberg
  (three volumes)
J. M. Synge
Ramón del Valle-Inclán
Frank Wedekind
Oscar Wilde

For a complete catalogue of Methuen Drama titles
write to:

Methuen Drama
50 Bedford Square
London
WC1B 3DP

or you can visit our website at:

www.methuendrama.com

Printed in the USA
CPSIA information can be obtained
at www.ICGtesting.com
LVHW020839171024
794056LV00002B/291